Winning the
Disability
Challenge

Winning the Disability Challenge

A Practical Guide to Successful Living

By John F. Tholen, Ph.D.

New Horizon Press
Far Hills, New Jersey

iv

New Horizon Press
P.O. Box 669
Far Hills, NJ 07931

John F. Tholen, Ph.D.
Winning the Disability Challenge:
A Practical Guide to Successful Living

Cover design: Robert Aulicino
Interior design: Ron Hart

Library of Congress Control Number: 2007936336

ISBN 13: 978-0-88282-290-7
ISBN 10: 0-88282-290-X
New Horizon Press

Manufactured in the USA

2012   2011   2010   2009   2008 / 5 4 3 2 1

Disclaimer

No book can replace the services of a trained physician. This book is not intended to cure or treat injury, illness, disease or any other medical problem by the layman. Any application of the recommendations set forth in the following pages is at the reader's discretion and sole risk.

Dedication

For Sandy—as wonderful an editor as she
is a wife, mother, nurse practitioner and attorney—
and our sons, Ben and Daniel. No father could
ask for more.

Author's Note

My awareness of physical impairment began in childhood, as I was born with a short left foot missing all five toes. My personal understanding of disability increased greatly in 1991, when I injured my back carrying my kids' playhouse to an upstairs deck. Although a major surgery was helpful, I now experience chronic pain and my activities are limited. Fortunately, I can perform my job as a psychologist as long as I can listen, think, write, and talk. If my work required any physical labor, I would need to find a new occupation. Unlike my clients, however, I only have to contend with all of the other challenges created by disability.

By far the greatest part of my education in the psychological impact of occupational disability has been provided by the many disabled men and women I've counseled over the course of the past twenty-seven years. In my attempts to help these many good people manage the psychological effects of their disabilities and reclaim greater control over their lives, I have gradually learned how life can be made successful even after becoming disabled. In order to preserve privacy and confidentiality, when discussing a particular patient, I used a fictitious name and altered any identifying characteristics.

It is my hope that through this book, I will be able to share information and ideas that can provide some relief to the many individuals who each year become overwhelmed by the stresses created by occupational or physical disability. Although it may be difficult to see from the midst of the crisis, it is almost always possible to make our lives better than had we never become disabled.

John F. Tholen, Ph.D.

Table of Contents

I

Introduction

After working hard for many years to support ourselves and our loved ones, injury or illness suddenly robs us of our capacity to work. We unexpectedly find ourselves faced with some very difficult questions: How are we to survive financially? Get proper medical care? Maintain our sense of self-worth? Fight off depression? Manage anxiety and worry? Resist the temptation to just give up?

This book attempts to provide some answers to the questions that confront and perplex millions of disabled Americans every day. The strategies presented herein have proven beneficial in the psychological treatment of thousands of disabled workers. By identifying reasons to be hopeful and finding sources of inspiration, we can generate the motivation necessary to constructively focus our time and energy. By adopting a philosophical view, expressing our feelings, making the most of important relationships, and nurturing our physical and emotional needs, we can meet even the most difficult challenges and establish a renewed sense of purpose and meaning.

What Most People Won't Understand

We are never prepared to become disabled. Until it does happen, most of us rarely even consider the possibility. We are all vulnerable, however, and when disability strikes, life can feel as if it has been suddenly turned upside-down. We find ourselves confronted with medical, legal, financial and emotional issues that are unfamiliar and often very confusing.

For most of us, life is hard enough under the best of circumstances. We are guaranteed many stresses in our lives. Some of us have survived traumatic childhood experiences or dysfunctional families, while others have been disappointed by a lack of physical attractiveness, athletic ability, academic skill or social popularity. People we care about will disappoint us. We will almost certainly experience conflicts with friends and family members. Our loved ones will age and someday will die. For those of us with children, they are likely to give us reason for anxiety. Health problems will trouble us and those we care about. The things we depend on, like our cars, houses and computers, will eventually break down. There will always be individuals that may attempt to cheat or harm us. There are always going to be people and events that annoy and inconvenience us. Becoming occupationally disabled, on the other hand, creates an entirely new set of problems that can make our previous troubles seem minor. Losing the ability to work is truly one of life's great insults. It presents us with the difficult challenge of finding new ways to support ourselves and fulfill personal goals. We suddenly can be confronted with the major task of finding new sources of security, meaning and peace of mind.

Few people who have not had the experience are likely to appreciate just how disruptive and stressful becoming disabled can be. Even if we are fortunate enough to receive a steady disability income, the amount rarely comes close to what we made when working. Reduced income can force us to make major lifestyle changes. Delays and interruptions of benefits can heighten our sense of helplessness. Even when the amount we receive is sufficient to meet our basic needs, few of us are comfortable depending on a government agency or insurance company. Furthermore, our benefits may suddenly or arbitrarily be reduced or discontinued. It is not too surprising that becoming disabled causes most of us to experience a major sense of insecurity.

If the diagnosis of our disabling medical condition is unclear or the source of our disability is not readily apparent to others, we can expect to hear skeptical comments from employers, coworkers and others who may have been exposed to sensationalistic media coverage of injury claim fraud. It is human nature to respond to misfortune in a way that helps them feel better, but which may be demoralizing to us. Sometimes doctors become annoyed with patients whose medical conditions do not respond well to treatment. Not even our closest friends and loved ones may be able to sustain support and understanding indefinitely, and may perhaps inadvertently say or do things that make us feel even worse.

Life Feels Different

Becoming disabled can be demoralizing and may result in a profound loss of motivation and direction in life. Viktor Frankl, a psychiatrist who had survived three years in a Nazi concentration camp, observed that becoming occupationally disabled can produce a similarly disorienting experience. It can create a similar sense of what Frankl calls "a provisional existence of unknown duration." This feeling makes it almost impossible to continue pursuing one's usual life goals. The easiest path may seem to be passive acceptance of just existing without goals, without a sense of the future, without the hope of accomplishing anything worthwhile and merely observing a working world that has become out of reach to us. Feelings of hopelessness can reduce us to a state of apathy, preventing exposure to the type of positive experiences that might alter our pessimistic outlook.

Although most of us like to complain about our jobs, the ways in which they help us cope with the demands of every-day life become very apparent when we are disabled. Whatever sense of accomplishment our work may have provided is suddenly gone, along with the camaraderie we enjoyed with co-workers, the gratification we felt at being part of a team effort to achieve something worthwhile, and the pride we felt in bringing home wages we had earned.

Losing the ability to work can also diminish our sense of self-worth. For many of us, self-esteem depends on our ability to produce in our occupation, earn a living and contribute to the support of our family. Becoming unable to work can magnify our normal self-doubts into some feelings of uselessness. Becoming disabled can raise some disturbing questions: What are we good for if we can't work? Of what use are we if we can't support our loved ones? What kind of future can we possibly look forward to as disabled workers?

Time Seems to Change

Prolonged disability can also alter our sense of time. For most of us, our job dictates the time we get up in the morning, when we go to bed at night and even when and what we eat for meals. From the time that we awaken in the morning until the time we arrive home at the end of the workday, our lives are largely dictated by our jobs. Upon becoming disabled, we can suddenly feel "lost" in time. Although a single day can seem endless, we can also be left with the sense that we are accomplishing little or nothing as the weeks of disability seem to fly by. Whereas it can feel wonderful to sleep late and relax on the weekend after a hard week at work or while on an earned vacation, when we become disabled we lose the contrast with working that makes our time off so enjoyable. One day of disability becomes like every other day of disability. Sleeping in begins to add to our growing sense of uselessness and weekends lose their special attraction. As G.B. Shaw observed, "A perpetual holiday is a good working definition of hell," especially when we are impaired.

Our Plans Disrupted

Disability can also shatter our illusions. Maybe we're not as tough as we like to think we are. We are forced to confront harsh realities: all of us are vulnerable, we're always getting older, we can't count on others to solve our problems and the world is far from perfect.

We may have expected that an employer would show

some loyalty to a hardworking long-term employee who has become disabled, especially if the disability arose because of a work-related injury or illness. Unfortunately, it seems that companies and government agencies are incapable of experiencing human emotions, and sadly, some of the people who run them do not seem to have the compassion and loyalty needed for such jobs. As a result, when we become disabled, we are sometimes treated like a machine part that has gone bad, replaced as quickly as possible with one that works. While this response may be understandable from a business point of view, it can leave those of us who become disabled feeling discarded and betrayed.

Losing the capacity to perform our jobs can severely disrupt the plans we have made for the future. It is entirely understandable that we may be expected to work many more years in our usual occupation and that we may even have planned to work for one particular employer until retirement. Unfortunately, the future often unfolds quite differently than we had anticipated or hoped and a disabling injury or illness may quickly make our plans irrelevant.

Disability can also deprive us of many activities that we have grown dependent on for entertainment and pleasure. We may lose our ability to walk the dog, work on the car, take care of the yard or play sports with our children or grandchildren. We may become unable to work out, keep the house clean, play golf, bowl, dance, move the furniture or engage in vigorous sexual activity. It is not surprising that we become preoccupied with our losses, frustrations and anxieties.

Disability can also disrupt even the most successful relationship. Its effects are likely to reverberate through the entire family. Our spouse or significant other is most likely to be particularly affected. New demands fall upon our able-bodied partner and activities that previously brought us closer together (dancing, traveling, bowling, sex, etc.) may become difficult or impossible. Adjusting to our disability is likely to eventually overtax our partner's capacity for compassion and understanding. With both our partners and ourselves under considerable stress, tensions can sometimes erupt into heated disagreements or quiet detachments. When nearly half of all marriages fail within seven years even when no disability is involved, it is not too surprising that the rate is even higher when one partner becomes demoralized by disability.

Powerful Emotions

Prolonged disability is often accompanied by powerful emotions that can be directed both inwardly and at others. We may feel angry at ourselves for having contributed to our disability in some way: lifting something too heavy, rushing or being careless, tolerating an unsafe or toxic work environment or putting our employer's demands ahead of our own health and safety.

Other times, our anger may be directed outward at a supervisor or co-worker who played some role in our becoming disabled, at a doctor whose treatment was lacking in some way or at an employer who "discarded" us once we lost our usefulness. Powerful feelings of anger can also be generated by the denial of disability claims, delays in the provision of reasonable benefits and the limitations of our legal and social support systems. Unfortunately, public agencies, officials' rules and insurance companies sometimes appear to be focused more on preventing an undeserving person from getting benefits than ensuring that they are received by a deserving person who may desperately need them.

Hope!

If we become occupationally disabled for more than a few weeks, we are likely to experience a wide variety of disturbing emotions. At times we may feel "pushed to the limit," ready to "snap," like "giving up," or as though we are "going crazy." As understandable as these disturbing feelings are, they are not the inevitable end result of disability. Twenty-seven years of counseling thousands of disabled workers and adjusting to my own disabilities have shown me that the adverse effects of disability can be overcome. Not only is there life after disability, but a disabled person can become more than just a survivor. My clients have repeatedly demonstrated that it is possible, with patience and persistence, to attain a rewarding and meaningful life even after becoming occupationally disabled. In this book, I will present strategies, suggestions, tips and approaches that can help any of us overcome the many challenges that almost always result from becoming disabled.

II

Taking Care of Business

For most of us, the first concern that will usually arise when we become disabled is how we are going to support ourselves and those who may depend on us if we are unable to work. In order to protect ourselves from extreme financial hardship and best prepare ourselves to begin tackling the psychological challenges, the best first step in responding to disability is almost always to apply for all potentially available monetary, medical and assistance benefits at the earliest possible time. Appendix A at the end of this book presents a "Guide to Disability Benefits and Rights" that discusses the various types of assistance that may be obtainable by those of us who have lost our capacity to work and whose financial security has become uncertain.

Although the disability benefits each individual qualifies for varies, applications should be submitted at the earliest time possible, including those for Social Security Disability Insurance (SSDI) or any long-term disability program that we may be covered by instead. Even if we are already receiving some other type of disability benefit, it is prudent to

apply for SSDI (or long-term disability). Although we may
not initially be entitled to a full benefit, these claims can
take many months to process. Having an SSDI claim
approved (or at least in progress) can be crucial to our
financial well-being if our temporary disability benefits,
such as those provided by worker's compensation and state
disability programs, are suddenly interrupted.

Appendix B is a state-by-state list of programs and
organizations that assist disabled individuals in obtaining
information, benefits, rehabilitation services and/or
protection of legal rights. Appendix C is a list of
organizations that may be able to assist individuals who are
affected by various chronic medical conditions.

Unless we have accumulated considerable savings or
other guaranteed sources of income, economizing will be an
important step in coping with occupational disability. If we
anticipate that our disability may be extended, we can begin
preparing to live as inexpensively as possible. We can
consider possibilities for obtaining less expensive housing
and transportation. We can consider taking in a boarder.
We can try to take pride in living on as little as possible. We
can avoid taking on new financial obligations. It is also wise
to avoid the cost of storing furniture and other possessions
if we relocate to a more economical residence. Although we
may prize our possessions and furniture—they are, after all,
just *things*—it may make the most sense to sell those
possessions that are not essential, with the plan of buying
replacements when we are in a better position to do so.

Once we have done what we can to adjust to the decline
in income that usually accompanies disability, we may be

able to turn our attention toward the psychological challenges that typically arise. Even when it seems that occupational disability has thrown a roadblock across the paths that we had planned for our lives, there are always other routes to explore, some of which may be even more rewarding than the ones we were on.

We can also attempt to accommodate lost capacities and/or reduced income by taking steps such as moving into a one-story or ground-level residence, finding less expensive living accommodations, seeking a handicap parking placard or disabled bus pass, shopping at stores that offer motorized ride-on carts, shopping at low-volume hours (or via the internet) in order to avoid crowds and delays, eliminating all non-essential expenses and exploring various pain management treatment modalities. We may also be able to form connections with others who have been through the disability experience in order to learn how they have managed in meeting similar challenges.

III

The Challenge

Although we are likely to experience a sense of helplessness, each of us who becomes occupationally disabled is presented with a choice:

Remain focused on what we have lost, and become resigned to feeling useless and helpless,

or

Face the challenges posed by disability, actively pursue other ways of feeling productive and attempt to carve out a rewarding life experience.

<u>Disability as a "Turning Point"</u>

Although becoming disabled can be distressing and demoralizing, we have the power to change it into a positive "turning point" in our lives. If we can find the inspiration and energy to strive forward, we can persist at exploring new possibilities.

Losing our ability to work can liberate us from a routine working existence that met our needs but also may have been holding us back, blocking us from making the most of our lives. Becoming disabled can free up time and energy that we can put to better use by actively pursuing goals that may have previously been unrecognized or neglected. After adjusting physically and economically, we can resolve each day to try to make it better and more meaningful than it would have been if we were still working. Surprising as it may seem, becoming disabled can be a wake-up call, the start of a more meaningful life and greater peace of mind.

Few jobs allow us to utilize our full potential or feel that we are accomplishing importance beyond bringing home a paycheck. But we often spend so much time and energy on our work that it can be difficult to find the time to address or pursue goals that might be even more important to us. Our jobs can become an excuse for our failure to make the most of our lives and for not actively pursuing our highest aspirations. I know this fact all too well, having spent the past thirty-five years being "too busy" working as a psychologist to test the possibility that if I could succeed as a writer, which was my true aspiration since I fell in love with John Steinbeck's books in eighth grade.

When we are working, we often have thoughts such as, *If only I had enough time I'd...help out at the kids' school...learn to operate a computer...spend more time with my sister...go back to college...learn to speak a foreign language...start up a home business...become an amateur pilot...try to write a book...learn to play the piano.* When we take a moment to examine ourselves as we were before we became disabled, we may see that we weren't making the most of our lives, living up to our greatest potential or making our personal relationships as positive as they could be. We might see that we haven't donated time to that social or political cause we feel so strongly about, tried our hand at all the crafts that appeal to us, sharpened our photography skills, learned a second language, painted on canvas, taken up a musical instrument, read the best books or become socially active. We sometimes use the fact that we are working to justify settling for less, failing to strive for what could be our most important goals. Our jobs can become excuses for limiting our life experiences and potential accomplishments. Becoming disabled holds the potential to "wake us up" to new possibilities.

No matter what our age, the time we have left in our lives is too precious to waste any more than is necessary on negative thoughts and emotions. Even when we feel "stuck" and "hopeless," we can begin working to alter those feelings by reviewing and rehearsing rational ideas. We can search for inspiration to push through the many obstacles that would keep us passive and withdrawn, and we can reach for what's best in ourselves and others. We can strive to paint our lives in the rich texture that can be found in satisfying, intimate relationships, constructive activity, helping others in need, as well as personal growth and accomplishment.

Becoming disabled can give us a chance to re-evaluate our priorities and move in new directions. We can try out new ways of relating to others. We can invest whatever energy we can muster in causes that are important to us and explore the limits of our remaining capacities. And we can investigate those aspects of life that have always interested us but have never pursued, possibly because our jobs consumed so much of our time and energy. Becoming disabled can be a "release" to begin acting more assertively and thinking more rationally in order to enrich our lives and the lives of those we love. Even those of us who have lost almost all physical capacities continue to have the potential to fully develop ourselves intellectually, philosophically and spiritually.

We do not make changes of this magnitude easily or overnight, but by persistently following the basic strategies presented in this book, the obstacles that are likely to arise as the result of our disability can be surmounted and the challenge can be won.

<u>Finding Opportunities Within the Crisis</u>

Although we are likely to consider an occupational disability to be a *catastrophe*, it is more reasonably viewed as a life *crisis*. The Japanese written character that represents the concept of "crisis" is actually a combination of two other characters; one that represents "catastrophe" and another that denotes "opportunity." Whereas catastrophe implies unavoidable ruin, crisis implies uncertainty and possibility. Catastrophe leads to hopelessness and apathy, but crisis calls for decision and action. Although becoming occupatio nally disabled may be a major life crisis, it doesn't have to be a catastrophe. As unlikely as it may seem, the crisis of disability can bring out the best in us, force us to make positive changes and lead to a rewarding life experience.

Although it's natural to hope our lives will go smoothly, it is by overcoming challenges that we grow and approach our full human potential. By surmounting adversity, we create a much greater sense of self-sufficiency and personal security than we could have developed had our lives followed an easier path. Disability is life's sternest challenge, but is also an opportunity for personal triumph and growth.

A large part of my work with disabled clients, many of whom have become preoccupied with their losses, is challenging them to identify the opportunities that continue to exist in their lives despite their disability, then providing support and guidance as they attempt to make the most of those opportunities. When clients tell me that they want everything to be "just like it was before I became disabled," I tell them that my goal for them is higher. I want them to someday be able to look back, feel grateful and think, *Thank God that happened to me; because if it hadn't, I would probably never have taken the path that got me to where I am today.* I tell them, "When I see a new client who doesn't see how they can survive the crisis of disability, I'll have that person talk to you so you can explain to them how it can be done."

We've Already Got What It Takes

Feeling overwhelmed by the demands of adjusting to occupational disability is an entirely normal experience. Sometimes we may feel that we just aren't capable of recovering from such an enormous loss, that we aren't smart enough, strong enough or clever enough—that we just don't have what it takes. This sense of hopelessness results from the fact that when we become discouraged, we often lose sight of both our own capacities and the resources that may be available. An important step in winning the disability challenge is recognizing that we do not have to change *who we are* in order to change *how we feel.* Each of us has the capacity to learn how to manage our own thoughts and actions sufficiently to create a rewarding life experience even after becoming disabled.

Even though we may not recognize it, each of us has everything we need to construct a successful disability "recovery" program. Because we are all different, the best disability "recovery" program for each of us is going to be one that we create for ourselves in order to fit our personal strengths, interests and preferences. Success is likely to require patience, persistence (even in the face of perceived failure) and a willingness to explore both ourselves and our available opportunities--but not that we become a different person. In fact, winning the disability challenge is far more likely to be the result of fully expressing and discovering the person that we already are. Although we may never be able to regain the working capacities we have lost, by tapping previously unused capacities and investing our time and energy in activities that are unaffected by our impairment, we can achieve a more rewarding life experience.

Persistence Pays Off

Surmounting the adversities of disability requires persistence in the face of frustration. Our progress is likely to be interrupted by setbacks and at those times it is normal to experience the illusion that we have accomplished nothing, which may cause us to feel like giving up. The truth, however, is that every effort made adds to the foundation of our eventual success. If we refuse to give up, these "setbacks" will pass, allowing us to once again see that progress is being made.

Persisting in the face of disappointment and what seems like "failure" is essential to ultimate success. The only way we can truly fail is by abandoning the quest. If we refuse to give up, repeatedly focus on our possible actions in the current moment and learn to "let go" of the setbacks and other concerns that are beyond our control, we can conquer the challenges presented by disability.

Viktor Frankl tells us that even prisoners in a Nazi concentration camp, who had good reasons to despair, were able to transcend their seeming hopelessness through acts of love and dignity. He witnessed internees lending support and encouragement to others who were on the verge of completely giving up, while making sacrifices to comfort the needier even at their own peril. If human beings in such demoralizing circumstances were able to find ways of demonstrating courage and creating positive experiences, then the goal of surviving and winning the disability challenge is clearly within the reach of us all.

Blessings and Possibilities

One of the first steps toward success in winning the disability challenge is identifying opportunities and possibilities that remain available to us. Although disability can cause us to become preoccupied with what we have lost, no matter how many limitations are imposed by our disability, we are always left with many blessings. Almost all of us who become disabled still have people we care about and who care about us. We usually have enough food, clothing and shelter. We usually still have our minds, sight and ability to express ourselves. We may still be able to appreciate the beauty of nature, the warmth of sunlight or the refreshment of a cool breeze. We still have our legal freedoms and rights. No matter how difficult it may become to see a future of success and fulfillment, many possibilities continue to exist. We may be able to obtain assistance to support ourselves and our families, secure affordable housing, train for a new occupation or start up a home business. We can always work at showing the people we care about how much we treasure them. And we may even be able to assist or comfort someone in greater need, contribute something meaningful to our family or inspire someone else.

Because we often have difficulty feeling thankful about anything after suffering a disabling injury or illness, it may be useful to take an inventory of those things for which we might continue to feel grateful (see Exercise 1). When we are so discouraged that we can't find anything to be grateful for, a close friend or loved one may be able to help us recognize that we still have things to be thankful about and opportunities to make our lives better. As time passes, we are likely to still recognize other reasons for gratitude. Attempting to build an "attitude of gratitude" in this way can eventually diminish our feelings of anger and grief.

When we first recognize that our disability may be pro-longed, it can seem that there is little or nothing left in the world that could make us feel useful or happy. This is an irrational idea, however, and can be challenged by drawing a map of our "Universe of Potential Positive Experience" (see Exercise 2). The sample "Universe" was produced by a client I'll call "Carl" who was feeling hopeless after becoming disabled by his chronic lumbar spine injury. Before he became disabled, Carl was an active person who spent much of his free time exploring the local mountains and playing sports with his friends and children. Losing his capacity to engage in those activities was difficult for Carl to accept. And when he suffered an emotional breakdown in the office of his orthopedic surgeon, he was referred for psychological consultation.

At my first meeting with Carl, he was preoccupied with the loss of so many of his favorite activities and confessed that he feared that he was doomed to lead a "miserable" existence in the future. By searching for activities he might enjoy that were not precluded by his injury, however, Carl saw that his future was not really hopeless. Even though his disability would restrict him from many activities, he was able to recognize that the number of things from which he might still gain enjoyment was limited only by his own imagination and willingness to explore new experiences.

Although each of us will generate a different graph of "possible" and "impossible" activities, the challenge for each of us is to shift the focus of our attention and energy from those activities that have been lost to the many that remain possible. Even when we may not be able to see any reason to be hopeful, our lives are never truly hopeless. If we are willing to search and to attempt new activities, we will always find some worth pursuing and some way to create more rewarding new life experiences.

EXERCISE 1

THINGS FOR WHICH I AM GRATEFUL

Loved Ones:

Good Friends:

Others Who Provide Emotional Support or Companionship:

Things I Like About Where I Live:

Comforts and Conveniences of My Home:

Prized Possessions:

Spiritual Faith/Connections:

Foods I Can Still Enjoy:

Hobbies and Interests I Can Still Pursue:

Sources of Financial Support:

EXERCISE 2

ONE PERSON'S UNIVERSE OF POTENTIAL POSITIVE EXPERIENCE

 Areas of potential positive experience which are no longer possible because of disability

 Areas of potential positive experience which remain possible despite disability

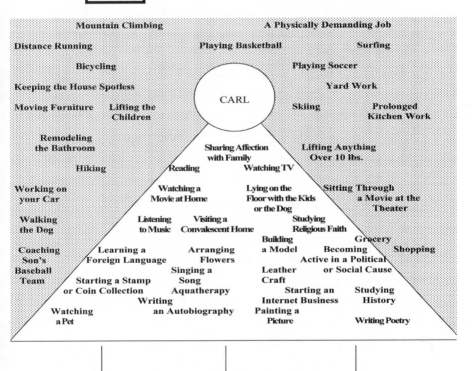

The number of our potential positive experiences is limited only by our imagination and willingness to try new things.

__Inspiration__

No matter how bad things may seem, we can almost always gain inspiration from others who have overcome disabilities and problems even more severe and difficult than our own. Three individuals, in particular, can serve as sources of inspiration, courage and hope.

Most of us know the story of the late actor, Christopher Reeve. Before becoming paralyzed from the neck down when thrown from a horse, he was a movie star best known for his lead role as *Superman*. After becoming profoundly disabled to the point that he had to re-learn how to breathe, Christopher Reeve became even more well-known for the amazing courage and fortitude he displayed in speaking out on behalf of severely impaired spinal injury patients everywhere. His valiant efforts have both contributed to the advancement of medical science in the area of spinal injury and have brought even greater respect and dignity to people with severe spinal injury. Christopher Reeve will live in our memories in a far more meaningful and inspirational way than would be the case had he never become paralyzed.

Stephen Hawking is one of the most eminent astrophysicists of our time, and one of the smartest men in the world. He has written and continues to write books that make the amazing complexities of our universe understandable even to those of us who are not scientists. He has achieved greatness despite the fact that he developed ALS, Lou Gehrig's disease, as a graduate student some twenty-five years ago. For many years, he has been completely paralyzed below the neck, dependent upon a mouth-controlled wheelchair to get around and utilizes a voice synthesizer to communicate. In recent years, Dr. Hawking also fell in love, got married and then divorced, just like people who have no disability at all. He refused to allow what most of us would consider a catastrophic disability to prevent him from fulfilling his potential, and this can serve as an inspiration to us all.

In the movie *My Left Foot*, Daniel Day-Lewis plays Christy Brown, an Irishman who was celebrated for his poetry and paintings, despite the fact that he was born without the ability to speak intelligibly or use any of his limbs except his left foot. Born into a large and poor Irish family and living on the floor of the small family home, Brown was cared for in every respect by his mother. Whereas virtually everyone believed that he was not only mentally challenged but also crippled, Brown's mother was convinced otherwise. Her conviction was confirmed when, at the age of eight, Brown finally managed to pick up a piece of charcoal with the toes of his left foot and scratch out a message on the floor. He later developed the capacity to use his left foot to paint works which have been acclaimed for their artistic value and even to write poetry, which he eventually became able to read aloud to large audiences.

And these three are not the only prominent people who have overcome major disabilities to make great accomplishments. Franklin Roosevelt was one of the most prolific United States presidents, despite being wheelchair bound much of the time. Senators Bob Dole and Daniel Inouye both enjoyed exemplary careers in public services despite disabling war injuries. Ron Kovic, whose life was chronicled in the movie *Born on the Fourth of July*, overcame a Vietnam War injury that left him paralyzed to become a congressman and political activist. And Theresa Saldana, the actress whose career was cut short by a near-fatal stabbing, subsequently anchored a nationwide movement to provide greater assistance to victims of violent crime.

While these individuals have possessed exceptional attributes, the fact that each was able to overcome a catastrophic disability to achieve something of major importance makes it clear that each of us is also capable of not only surviving, but of triumphing over our own limitations. Over the course of the past twenty-seven years, I have witnessed hundreds of inspiring, if less celebrated, successes by people more like you and me.

By her ninth unsuccessful surgery, one of my clients, Joanne, had permanently lost much of her ability to use either arm or hand due to severe nerve damage. It had become clear that she would not be able to resume her usual job as a keyboard operator, and she wondered what she might ever be able to do. Even brushing her teeth had become difficult. When I first saw Joanne, she was immersed in feelings of helplessness that were keeping her withdrawn and inactive. In treatment, however, Joanne was eventually able to recognize that, although she had lost a great deal, her life was not hopeless and that there might still be goals worth pursuing.

Although she was no longer capable of the extensive hand work necessary to resume her longtime doll making hobby, she discovered that she was still capable of making a different type of molded plastic doll. Eventually she had the opportunity to train as a Drug and Alcohol Counselor, a line of work she found rewarding because of a family history of substance abuse. The possibility of pursuing a new career in which she would be helping others was exciting to Joanne and her feelings about her disability slowly began to change. She became increasingly hopeful about her future and more open to trying new things. She began trying out a digital camera that had been sitting unused in her home for many months and discovered great pleasure in both taking pictures and in digitally manipulating the images she captured. Joanne's change of attitude was also a great relief to her husband and greatly benefited their marriage, which had become strained due to her despondency and irritability.

Another client, Steven, was also feeling helpless when I first saw him. A back injury had derailed his career as a diesel mechanic. Suddenly thrust into an unfamiliar world of doctors and lawyers, he had become almost completely passive, wishing things would change and waiting for someone else to change them. Once in treatment, Steven began to see that his best chance for future success would come from his own efforts rather than waiting for future medical and legal decisions, and he began actively exploring his options. He recalled that, while in college, he had aspired to become an attorney. Feeling that nothing could be lost, Steven set about completing a few courses that were still necessary to earn his undergraduate degree. Further motivated by this success, Steven studied hard for the law school aptitude test and scored high enough to gain admission to a local law school. By the time he was awarded a vocational retraining benefit through his legal case, Steven had just one year of law school left. Although the retraining benefitted his occupation, becoming an attorney was quite a great accomplishment for Steven. And to think, it might never have occurred had he not become disabled and then actively confronted his disability challenge.

After several years of working in a stressful middle management position, Mary became disabled by what initially seemed to be a relatively minor back injury. Within a few weeks, however, she had also developed widespread pain over much of her body, chronic fatigue, insomnia, headaches and forgetfulness. Suspecting some type of systemic disorder, Mary's doctor referred her to a rheumatologist, who eventually offered her a diagnosis of fibromyalgia, a poorly understood but highly disabling syndrome. By the time I first saw Mary, she had become completely preoccupied with the "catastrophic" effects of her illness and was talking as though her life was over.

Treatment helped Mary begin focusing her attention on how she might best expend her limited remaining energy. Becoming connected with other fibromyalgia sufferers through an internet website provided Mary with support and encouragement. She also benefited from what they had discovered about managing their symptoms. Mary began organizing her time in a way that assured her plenty of rest, but also included frequent, brief visits with the grandchildren she adored. She decided to discuss her condition with her minister and was persuaded to begin participating in some church groups and working to develop her spiritual faith. She began crocheting and donated the items she produced to church fundraising sales. In addition, she persuaded her husband to sit down with her and their minister and the expressions of mutual commitment that emerged helped to bridge the distance that had developed between them since the onset of Mary's disabling medical condition. Mary continues to be occupationally disabled, but she has discovered that her life is far from over.

Jerry was a very personable man who had worked in the city sewer system for years. A major shoulder injury combined with a childhood impairment of his other arm left him unable to even remove a manhole cover. This circumstance also caused Jerry to become despondent and worried. Once he was able to begin focusing on potential opportunities, however, Jerry began once again playing the guitar he had loved in his youth. He also found enjoyment in spending more time caring for and playing with his dog, and even started dating a woman he recognized in the supermarket as someone he had known in high school. Jerry was eventually able to begin real estate school and now works as an agent for a nationwide real estate brokerage. He reports that for the first time ever, he has a job he enjoys.

As a city building inspector, Dorothy had been battling male construction superintendents for years. Although she was initially distraught when a work injury caused her to become occupationally disabled during treatment, she had gradually realized that her disability might allow her to move in a more positive direction. She was gradually able to start up a personal services business that caters to a large senior citizens' community near her home. Dorothy reports that taking elderly people shopping, walking their dogs and even combing their horses provides much greater peace of mind than she had ever experienced while in her former job, from which she decided to retire early.

Joe lost one eye and suffered mild brain damage when part of his skull was crushed in an industrial accident. Then, while straining to do his best during tests of his remaining cognitive capacities, he suffered a heart attack. When I first examined Joe he was despondent. Although he had been a multi-skilled carpenter, he had discovered that he was no longer able to even complete simple repairs in his home. I gave Joe the assignment of snapping together a small Lego toy kit. His success at this simple task was gratifying to both of us, and he began attempting more difficult tasks. By gradually taking on tasks of increasing difficulty, Joe experienced numerous successes and became much more optimistic. He is currently working a few hours each day to refurbish an old motor home, in which he plans to visit family members scattered from coast to coast. He's once again excited about the possibilities in his future.

One of the clients I have most admired is Al, a fifty-nine-year-old man who successfully adjusted to a major loss of income after becoming disabled by injuries sustained in a traumatic assault. Limited to just under $900 per month in disability income, Al was able to rent an apartment for $300 per month through HUD's Section 8 housing program, obtain medical care through Medicaid insurance, obtain public transportation at a major discount for the disabled and get housekeeping and home health care services through a state program. He further economized by frequenting community food banks. Once he had constructed a lifestyle that fit his budget, Al then pursued his passions. Piece by piece he built an elaborate model train system that ran throughout his apartment. He then carved and painted miniature buildings, trees and people that made the train set come alive for him. Al acquired a pet cockatiel and trained it to respond to his verbal prompts with humorous quips. Finally, he wooed and wed his female housekeeper. Disability was clearly not the end of Al's life.

There are hundreds of similar success stories about individuals whose lives seemed to spin out of control when they became disabled, but were eventually able to focus on possibilities and opportunities and gradually rebuild a meaningful and rewarding life.

I have seen many disabled clients who had become despondent and hopeless, but were able to turn their lives around and achieve successes that might otherwise never have been possible. I recently read that one former client had become the executive director of a large environmental conservation coalition. I have followed a number of former clients through newspaper accounts of their active involvement in local government and politics. One client told me that her volunteer work at a local AIDS hospice had become the most rewarding experience of her life. I once attended a motivational seminar only to find that the principal speaker was a former client who, when I first saw her, had been completely hopeless and helpless after having become disabled.

These success stories demonstrate that becoming occupationally disabled does not put an end to our opportunities in life. The possibility of accomplishment and enjoyment continues to exist even after we become disabled. Despite our disability, we continue to have opportunities to expand and deepen relationships, test our capacities in previously untried pursuits and expose ourselves to potentially rewarding aspects of the world that we may have previously neglected. By exploring these possibilities we can reclaim our lives and open the door to a far richer and more meaningful life. This is what it means to win the disability challenge.

IV

Recognizing Where Our Power Lives

Most things that happen in this world are completely beyond our control as individuals: the ups and downs of the economy, political strife and wars, natural and man-made disasters or who wins the pennant or the presidency. Even many aspects of our own lives are beyond our control: the family into which we are born, the opportunities and resources available in the place where we grow up, our inherited weaknesses and even the actions of the people we care about most. We are saved from being helpless victims by one critical fact:

Each of us has considerable control over how we spend our energy in the current moment.

We are almost never completely powerless. Even when we feel most helpless we can usually still identify some current moment action that might make us feel better. By focusing our attention on how we expend energy in the current moment, we can exercise what power we have and we can gradually alter our experience of life. As the winds of circumstance and fortune buffet us on the sea of life, we can at least swim in the direction that promises the greatest hope of fulfilling our wishes and dreams. And in doing so, we can increase the respect we have for ourselves.

Each time we take action in the hope of improving our life experience in some way, our sense of helplessness is slightly diminished and our self-respect is slightly enhanced. Actions of this type communicate the message that our feelings count, that we are worth the effort. The more we are able to focus our energy on what we can do in this moment and in this day, the more we are able to release our emotional investment in everything else, and the greater our peace of mind will be. In this manner, it is possible to surmount the challenges that life seems to repeatedly put before us.

One Day at a Time

The current moment is the only time we have the ability to do anything. We have no power to control yesterday or tomorrow. Most of us recognize that we cannot change what has already happened. Although less obvious, it is just as true that we cannot reach out into the future and make it be as we would wish. "Now" provides our only opportunity to exercise our free will. The only way we can exert any control over the past or the future is by identifying, and then attempting to carry out some current moment action that might alter our thoughts and feelings about past events or future possibilities. The more time and energy we spend feeling distressed about the past or the future, the greater will be our sense of helplessness. Conversely, the more time and energy invested in current moment choices and actions, the more powerful and confident we are likely to feel.

The motto of Alcoholics Anonymous, one of the most respected recovery programs of our time, is "One Day at a Time." Learning to live more in the current moment and less in the past and future can be the key to "recovering" from either alcoholism, neurosis, psychological trauma or just about any other collapse of the human spirit. Unless some constructive current moment action is inspired, focusing our attention on past regret or future worry can cause emotional stress and feelings of helplessness, which may trigger self-defeating, emotion-numbing behavior such as drinking alcohol excessively.

The Past and the Future

The past is over and done with, written in stone. Although our memories of and feelings about the events that occurred in the past will change over time, we have no power at all to change what has already taken place. Spending time and energy on feelings of remorse or anger can make us feel helpless because we *are* completely helpless with respect to changing the past. We can influence past events only by taking some action in the current moment that might change our feelings about those events. We can write about them, talk to someone about them, attempt to make amends, strive to forgive ourselves or others, build a memorial, resolve to do better, express our feelings creatively, dedicate ourselves to a cause, etc. Though we will never be able to change what has already taken place, no matter how much we may rehash painful memories, by taking actions of this type in the present moment we can alter our feelings about the past.

Although it is less immediately obvious, we also have no control in the future. We cannot reach out in time and make events unfold according to our wishes. Unless we are inspired to take some constructive current moment action, spending time and energy worrying about the future is as pointless as dwelling in remorse or anger about the past, and is just as likely to make us feel helpless. Anxiety about the future can be useful only if we are able to translate it into some current day action that might make us feel more comfortable or optimistic about what may come in the future. For example, in response to worries about the future, we might enroll in a class, send out a resume, start an exercise program, make an appointment, install a security system or find a less expensive place to live. Just making a list of goals to accomplish can improve our sense of control and diminish our anxiety. By repeatedly taking action on a moment-to-moment, day-by-day basis, we may be able to both alter our feelings about the future and increase the likelihood that it will unfold in a manner we would prefer.

Choices

The choices we make today represent our only means of influencing our lives and how we feel about them. Although it may sometimes seem that our actions are dictated by circumstances or the demands and needs of others, in truth, we are almost continuously confronted with choices about how to spend our limited time and energy. We may choose to make a phone call, write a letter, take a walk or drive, confront a friend, take a nap, pet the dog, read a book, listen to some music, see a movie, consult a professional, search for information on the internet and so on. Although disability may rob us of many options in life, the list of our potential actions remains almost infinite. When disability closes some doors to us, we can almost always find others to open. We can attempt to follow Coach John Wooden's advice and not let what we can no longer do stop us from doing what we still can. By using the current moment to attempt some kind of constructive action, we can enhance our self-confidence, self-respect and peace of mind.

Whether we recognize it or not, we are constantly making choices that affect the quality of our lives. The more time and energy we devote to making and carrying out current moment choices, the less helpless we are likely to feel. Conversely, the more time and energy we spend on distressing thoughts of the past or anxious worry about the future, the more helpless we are likely to feel. The goal, each day, should be to identify and carry out as many constructive and positive actions as we are able, forgive ourselves for whatever we did not manage to accomplish and then release whatever distressing thoughts remain. In this way we can improve the quality (and feel more in charge) of our own life experience.

Distressing thoughts about either the past or the future are best managed by "translating" them into current moment actions. When feeling distressed we can ask ourselves, "What are my choices at this moment? What can I do now that might make me feel better?" For example, if we are distressed about a recent conflict with a friend, a past event that we have no power to alter, then we might decide to telephone that person, send a card or even speak to a mutual friend about helping to resolve the conflict. If we are upset about losing the ability to run, we can check out the local facilities for swimming or see if riding a bicycle might be possible. Even those of us who become paraplegic may be able to exercise or even compete in a swimming pool or a racing wheelchair. If we are despondent about losing the ability to compete in tennis matches, we may find it possible to compete in contests of darts, bocce, bowling, cards or even video games.

When I became concerned that changes in insurance company practices would have a negative impact on my psychology practice, I sought out more information, made appointments to talk to friends who might have good ideas about rebuilding a practice, began contacting new referral sources and started outlining this book.

The goal is always to identify actions in the current moment and current day that are likely to make us feel all the better about distressing past events or frightening future possibilities, and then invest as much time and energy in taking those steps as we can. In doing so, we can minimize self-defeating feelings of helplessness and powerlessness by shaping our own life-experience and enhancing our own self-confidence.

Letting Go and Turning Over

Unfortunately, there is no guarantee that our attempts at constructive action will bring us peace of mind. Even after we have taken every positive step we can think of, we may continue to be troubled by intrusive and distressing thoughts of the past or the future. Most of us are capable of repeatedly "beating ourselves up" for having failed to accomplish some goal, and/or feeling perpetually terrified of the possible catastrophes that might strike our lives at any time. The solution to this dilemma is to recognize when thoughts that distress us have become, at least for the moment, completely out of our control, they are best released, "let go" or "turned over," so that they do not continue to cause us to feel helpless.

When we can no longer find any constructive action that might alter our feelings about a troubling event or circumstance, that event or circumstance ceases to be our business at least for that moment. Our challenge, then, is to find some way to "let go" or "turn over" the distressing thought to whosever business it may actually be: an attorney, doctor, relative, employer or some other individual. If no other person can be identified as responsible for taking care of the problem, and we've done all that we can think of to do, it may be time to invoke some higher power. Faith in a Supreme Being can assist in, but is not absolutely essential to mastering the "letting go/turning over" process. It can be easier to maintain peace of mind if we consider all things that are outside of our current day control to be in "God's control" or "God's business," part of a divine plan that is a mystery to us. It makes sense to "turn over" to God responsibility for what only God can control. Failing to do so and hanging on to distressing thoughts about events outside our control may be seen as an indication that we are confusing ourselves with God, acting as though we have some divine power or control. Many individuals who do not possess a strong religious faith have been able to achieve a similar "letting go" process, by "turning over" those aspects of life that can't be controlled to a generalized concept of a higher power, such as the "great mystery" of the universe, or even to a "future day."

The "turning over" process can be difficult to master, especially for those of us who tend to worry obsessively. While obsessive-compulsive tendencies can prevent us from overlooking something that may be important, they can also cause us to just torture ourselves with pointless worry and concern. I've had many obsessive-compulsive clients tell me that living "one day at a time" did not initially work for them. They found it necessary to live "five minutes at a time," as they would repeatedly turn over ineffectual thoughts and worries, only to find that they returned a few minutes later.

In order to avoid being plagued by pointless remorse and anxiety, each of us faces the same challenge: finding some method of releasing distressing thoughts and worries over which we have no control. Many individuals have found it helpful to recite the "Serenity Prayer", which is often attributed to German theologian Reinhold Niebuhr, but reflects a philosophy that dates back to ancient Roman philsophers:

"God grant me the serenity to accept the things I cannot
change, the courage to change the things I can,
and the wisdom to know the difference."

I have one devoutly Christian client who benefits from frequently reminding herself that "there is a divine solution to every problem." Her strong faith helped her to better manage her anxiety by making it easier for her to "turn over" to God her fears about the future. Each of us is capable of improving our ability to accept those aspects of life that we cannot change. Refusing to do so would be as nonsensical as repeatedly crashing into an immovable barrier rather than looking for a way around it.

During difficult times, many of us are inclined to pray for changes in the circumstances of our lives that trouble us. Rather than take responsibility for changing our own thoughts and feelings, it is tempting to pray for miraculous healing or a sudden windfall. It is often easier to remain passive and miserable than to actively pursue a constructive change. When we pray for strength and guidance to set ourselves right and for help in "letting go" of what we can't possibly control, we are seeking inner peace. In my view, the great gift of faith is that it allows us to call on a higher power to inspire us to persevere in our attempts at constructive action, and helps to relieve us from responsibility for the many aspects of life that are out of our control. When we have taken every constructive current moment action that we can identify, we can seek greater peace of mind by turning over our remaining anxieties to a higher power. When a person of strong spiritual faith is persistently troubled by anxiety, it is probably a sign that his or her faith could be more effectively practiced.

Today and Not Today

The sum of our moment-to-moment life experiences determines the quality of our lives. Our experience is constructed by our actions in a procession of current moments.

We possess no other power to influence the quality of our lives except that which we can exercise in the current moment and current day. And the actions of today shall lay the foundation for the choices that will be available to us tomorrow.

All of our potential actions can be divided into two basic and distinct categories: "Today" and "Not Today." When we postpone a potentially constructive or positive action until "tomorrow," "next week," or even "until I'm feeling better," the most significant point is that we are choosing to not perform that action today. If we don't manage to complete a particular action that we had planned for "Today," that action is automatically transferred to the "Not Today" category.

Forgiving Ourselves and Others

In order to devote our best effort to creating a more rewarding life experience, it will be helpful if we can find a way to forgive both ourselves and others. Because we are all human, we are all vulnerable to injury and inclined to make mistakes. Yet many of us feel guilty about, and become ashamed of, the fact that we have become disabled. We may blame ourselves for being inattentive or clumsy, lifting something too heavy, repeatedly returning to a toxic work environment, driving too fast, failing to use adequate safety equipment or even trusting another person who let us down. Our mistakes, however, are best viewed not as signs of personal inadequacy, but rather as reflections of the fact that, like all human beings, we are far from perfect. Even when we have the best intentions we're destined to make mistakes.

We stumble. We bump into things. We forget things. We require "down time." Our minds wander. It can seem to take us forever to get something done. The fact that we sometimes "screw up" does not make us inferior or less deserving than others; it simply makes us human.

The world is a vast and mysterious place. Our lives are difficult. We're given no instruction manual. We are poor at predicting the future. We have little control over many events that affect us profoundly. We are repeatedly forced to make decisions based upon limited information and without knowing how events will actually unfold. Although we rarely take action without an honest hope of some positive outcome, it's hardly surprising that we often misstep. Only in retrospect are we able to see that another course of action might have been more successful.

Even our most well-meaning actions, at times, can in fact produce adverse outcomes. There are occasions when all humans act in ways that later seem foolish or inconsiderate. This is simply an inescapable aspect of human life. When things go wrong after we become disabled, attempting to forgive ourselves and others for being human may be the first step toward managing the guilt and/or anger that can distract us from the work of remodeling our lives.

The only rational or constructive remedy for self-blame and guilt is to search for a way to atone, attempt to learn from our mistake and then forgive ourselves and "let it go," "turn it over" to a higher power or release it to the mystery of life. Our disability is the result of being human and being limited in our understanding of present circumstances and our ability to predict or control the future. Like most of life's traumas, becoming disabled is usually a consequence of living in a world that does not respect the concept of "fairness," where we are always vulnerable to injury or illness, and where we have little or no control over forces that can affect us profoundly. It would be best if we could view ourselves as innocent victims of misfortune, while at the same time recognizing that we still have considerable power to influence the quality of our life experience.

Although the aggressive expression of anger can be an obstacle to progress and recovery, anger is a very powerful emotion that we may be able to use to motivate us to take constructive action. The desire to gain revenge for perceived wrongs is entirely natural. If we can produce no more constructive response than seething internally and fantasizing about violence, then anger becomes self-defeating. When we harbor a grudge against another person, we allow that individual to continue to exert control over our own life experience. It is as though someone has wounded us and our response is to then repeatedly hurt ourselves in that person's memory.

The only "good revenge" is to respond to perceived wrongs at the hands of others by making our lives better. By using our anger to inspire constructive action and bolster our determination to persist until we succeed, we can enhance our sense of mastery over both our life circumstances and the basic impulses of human nature. By improving our lives, we demonstrate that the offending individual has had no real power to harm us. By containing our impulses, we can demonstrate the best of human nature. The less time and energy we devote to blaming or trying to get even with another person, the more time and energy we have available to invest in actions designed to promote our recovery from the emotionally traumatic effects of disability.

Medical science has verified what doctors have known for decades: *Ineffectual anger* that leads to destructive action only damages our health and shortens our lives. Anger can be constructive only when it is converted into energy and translated into positive action. Although taking revenge by harming another may be only briefly gratifying, destructive action damages both our target and ourselves. It turns us from victim to villain, and leaves us and everyone we care for living in a slightly nastier world.

Serene acceptance, on the other hand, allows us the best chance of solving the problems before us and promotes our own health and the well-being of those we love. We can improve ourselves and the world in which our children will live by redirecting our angry energy to some constructive purpose, and accepting and forgiving the actions of others as merely a reflection of their imperfection and weakness. Although it may seem easier to hate, it's healthier and ultimately more rewarding to forgive and accept.

One of the most attractive aspects of Christianity is the belief that all of our sins may be forgiven if we honestly repent. If God can be all-forgiving, perhaps it is possible for us to forgive ourselves for outcomes we never intended to produce, and others for harmful actions that resulted from their own human weaknesses and failings. Even when the actions of others upset us, we can recognize that they are merely a reflection of the human imperfection that exists in all of us, and we can attempt to be tolerant and forgiving.

V

Putting Things Into Perspective

Our emotional state, whether jubilant or despondent, tranquil or terrified, can depend as much on how we interpret the events and circumstances of our lives as on the events and circumstances themselves. Life has a way of repeatedly throwing obstacles into our path: trauma, loss, disappointment, injury, illness and sometimes the loss of our ability to work. Coping successfully with these challenges can depend upon our ability to both view our circumstances and ourselves rationally, to recognize that although our problems may be difficult, they are not insurmountable and that we possess the capacity to adjust and thrive in spite of them. Learning to manage our counterproductive patterns of thought can be the key to generating sufficient hope and motivation to rebound from the trauma of becoming disabled and to recreate a fulfilling and meaningful life.

Both our lives and disabilities can be viewed in many different ways. Although we rarely recognize the fact, we choose which view to accept. This power of choice provides us with the ability to control our emotions, attitudes and actions. Our challenge is to find and adopt a constructive and rational view that will generate sufficient hope and motivation to permit us to carve out a rewarding life *within the limitations and difficulties created by our disabilities.*

By learning to identify the counterproductive thoughts that cause our distress and block our progress, then introducing and repeatedly rehearsing more rational and constructive alternatives, we can improve our perspective and spur ourselves to a healthier course of action. By adopting a perspective on ourselves and our disabilities that makes us feel more optimistic and inspired, we will be able to see ourselves in a more favorable light, accomplish more and make our lives more rewarding.

Self-Talk: "Choosing" Our Emotions

We do not have control over our immediate emotional reactions to stressful life events. Our first reaction is the product of primitive processes centered deep in our involuntary nervous system. Just a split second later, however, we have the power to engage our cognitive processes and to begin rationally re-interpreting the event that occurred. This ability to filter our emotional reactions through our cognitive processes before we act allows us to respond based on mature reason rather than primitive emotion.

For example, when forced by a careless driver to suddenly swerve or brake, we're more likely to immediately experience intense fear and anger. Whereas our immediate impulse might be to somehow punish the offending driver, once we're able to engage our reasoning processes, we will recognize that the idea of acting on this impulse would be counterproductive. Rational reflection can allow us to see that the aggressive action would be unlikely to accomplish anything constructive and would almost certainly place both ourselves and others at risk. We may also be able to reason that we are likely to feel better about ourselves if we act in a reasonable and mature manner, rather than sinking to the level of immaturity shown by the offending driver. By learning to consciously engage our rational thought processes each time we become emotionally distressed about life events, we can both improve the quality of our experience and enhance our motivation to take constructive action.

Although we are often unaware, we silently "talk" to ourselves almost continuously. The content of our "self-talk," the stream of thought that passes through our minds most of our waking hours, has a lot to do with how we feel and the actions we take. If we tell ourselves that our circumstances are catastrophic or we belittle our capacity to cope, the resultant emotional pain and sense of hopelessness is likely to drain our motivation and energy, and impede our attempts at constructive action. On the other hand, if we can remind ourselves that many people have successfully coped with occupational disability and that we have survived all of the previous challenges of our lives and will most likely survive this crisis as well, we may feel more optimistic and motivated. By manipulating our self-talk, we have the power to alter our viewpoints, emotional experience and actions. We can choose to change our perspective, to reinterpret what has happened to us in a way that will make us feel better and become better able to move forward.

Our irrational thoughts are easiest to identify when we

are experiencing highly unpleasant emotions, when we're acutely anxious, panicky, angry or depressed. At those moments we can assess ourselves by asking, "What am I telling myself right now that may be causing these kinds of bad feelings?" Our goal is to identify and record the negative thoughts about ourselves and our circumstances that underlie our distressing emotions, so that we can then develop a more rational and positive alternative for each. If we have trouble recognizing the negative thoughts that underlie our emotional distress, then talking about our thoughts and feelings with a trusted and caring family member or friend (or even a professional cognitive-behavioral therapist) may be useful.

If we find that we're upset because of thoughts such as:

"I'll be useless if I can't get back to work"
or
"My future is ruined by this injury,"

we may generate more positive, rational alternatives such as:

"Even with my physical limitations, there are hundreds of ways that I can be more useful (e.g., as a mate, parent, grandparent, child, sibling, friend, companion, driver, volunteer, cook, mender, hobbyist, craftsperson, etc.) than when I was working,"
or

"If I can take this opportunity to begin developing my spirituality, learning more about the things that interest me, exploring new ways of being creative, spending more quality time with my loved ones and contributing time to the causes I think are important, my future will probably be better than if I'd never been injured."

Hopeless views, such as:

"I'll never feel better"
or
"I won't be able to survive,"

can be countered with more rational alternatives like:

"I've already overcome many obstacles and survived many challenges in the past, and with persistence and patience, I'll get through this one as well"
or
"Like all human beings, I'm capable of surviving and bouncing back"

or even

"I really don't have a choice; the people I care about are counting on me to cope with this, so I guess I'll have to."

A recurrent self-belittling idea like:

"I am a loser"

or

"I'm good for nothing,"

can be countered by more rational, alternative ideas such as:

"I do the best I can in a confusing
and difficult world"

or

"Though I have my share of human faults and
weaknesses, I am always trying to do what seems to be
for the best."

We can consciously alter our perspective by recording our self-defeating thoughts, developing constructive, rational alternatives for each one and then reviewing the constructive alternative whenever the self-defeating thought threatens to impede our progress. Small index cards provide one convenient method for recording both our negative thoughts and positive alternatives. When a self-defeating negative idea is identified, it can be written on one side of the card. Then, after we have developed a more rational replacement idea, it can be written on the opposite side. The list of rational affirmations at the end of this chapter can serve as examples of rational, alternative ideas. The cards can then be carried in a wallet or purse for easy reference. Each time the negative thought troubles us, we can refer to the card and rehearse the positive alternative until we experience some emotional relief. With repeated use of this approach, we can become increasingly familiar with more positive ways of viewing the circumstance. Eventually, this constructive substitution may be so well remembered that the cards are no longer needed.

Although our long-standing habits of thinking are unlikely to change easily or quickly, by repeatedly reviewing and rehearsing healthier positive ideas, we have the power to gradually alter our beliefs, attitudes, emotions and behavior. This ability can be a powerful resource in our efforts to cope with disability, as even small changes in our habits of thought can create greater optimism and energy.

How Severe Is This Crisis?

Another way to alter our perspective on a disturbing circumstance or event is to rate its severity on a scale from zero to ten, where zero represents no stress or trauma at all, and ten represents the greatest possible trauma we can imagine. In the moment, our crisis may seem catastrophic. When considered in the light of all possible traumas and losses, however, most of the things that cause us to become "stressed-out" are not so disastrous. Each time we find ourselves feeling that an event or circumstance of life is overwhelmingly stressful, we may benefit by comparing it against other stresses that people have survived. For example, in the eighteenth century the average Russian couple gave birth to thirteen children, only four of whom survived to the age of eighteen. When compared with the trauma resulting from losing nine children, our current problems may take on a less catastrophic perspective.

Reforming Our Prejudices

Some of us were programmed by our life experiences to belittle our abilities and to view events and circumstances of our lives in an unreasonably pessimistic light. This type of habitual, negative thinking is a normal reaction to a long history of disrespect and misfortune. Although it may seem to protect us from disappointment, it can also cause a great deal of unnecessary emotional distress and may impede our attempts to take constructive action to meet the challenges of disability. Fortunately, the same method that can transform our self-talk can prevent our actions from being controlled by counterproductive and utterly irrational self-prejudices.

Although the constitution we inherit from our parents plays a large part in determining our temperament (i.e., whether we tend to be fiery or easy-going), our feelings and beliefs about ourselves, and the messages that tend to reverberate in our minds as a result, often have more to do with what we have been repeatedly told by the important people in our lives as we were growing up. If we have been consistently exposed to a particular message, it is likely to become firmly entrenched in our own patterns of thought and may then be automatically replayed whenever we face a major challenge or stress. If the message is one of self-disparagement (e.g., "I am a loser" or "I can't do anything right") or helplessness (e.g., "What I do won't make any difference"), we are unlikely to fully invest ourselves in attempting to surmount the challenge. We are simply too intelligent to expend great energy on a task that we believe to be hopeless.

When we recognize a counterproductive self-prejudice, we can challenge it with a more rational and constructive viewpoint. By repeating this pattern each time the self-defeating idea intrudes into our thinking, we can reduce our sense of helplessness and improve the effectiveness of our responses.

Sometimes it can be helpful to remind ourselves that we already have a "track record" of at least some success in life. In order to have progressed to the current point in our lives, virtually every one of us has already met and overcome numerous challenges. The fact that we have survived every test that life has previously thrown in our path demonstrates that we possess the resiliency required to survive a life crisis such as becoming occupationally disabled. It may help to compile an inventory of both those things that we have managed to accomplish in our lives and all the difficulties we've had to overcome in order to do so. By making a list of our past successes (e.g., in school, by becoming self-taught, as a worker, by becoming self-sufficient, by forming strong relationships, as a parent, as a spouse, as a friend, in special interests, etc.) and the obstacles we refused to let stop us (family problems, lack of resources, learning disorders, physical disadvantages, illness, earlier traumas and losses, etc.), we can remind ourselves of our toughness and adaptability, and increase our sense of hopefulness. If we overcame those obstacles and achieved those successes in the past, we can overcome the challenges posed by disability.

The human mind seems to be prone to the development of prejudices, including those about ourselves. We may have developed the notion that we are lazy, too sensitive, undisciplined, "good-for-nothing" or even "doomed to fail." The stress of becoming disabled can magnify these self-prejudices and leave us feeling even less capable of coping with a crisis. Left unchecked, self-derogatory ideas can negatively color our view of every difficult circumstance we encounter and can prevent us from responding effectively. Fortunately, as adults, we are capable of "reforming" our self-prejudices and managing self-defeating patterns of thought. We can learn to recognize when counterproductive messages begin to reverberate in our minds and actively oppose them with constructive rational alternatives. We can become so aware of our own self-defeating habits of thought that we delay our responses until we have duly considered a more rational perspective. The process can happen like this:

At the age of forty-five, Carolyn sustained a neck injury that caused her to experience increasingly severe pain whenever she engaged in any physical activity, including most of the homemaking responsibilities that she had excelled in performing for many years for her family of five. It was her long-held belief that as a wife and mother, the state of her family and home were her responsibility, which reflected on her worth as a person. This conviction led her to continue her usual household routines despite the fact that these activities frequently caused her neck pain to become excruciating. Carolyn found herself becoming increasingly angry at her husband and children, who seemed comfortable allowing her to continue to care for them even though doing so caused her additional pain. Carolyn eventually recognized that the ideas she had incorporated early in her life--that a wife and mother should always be the one who takes care of the home and family, and that her value as a person depended on her doing so better than anyone else -- was just irrational and self-defeating. Since this rule was so firmly implanted in her habitual thinking, it continued to be Carolyn's first impulse to do whatever needed to be done, no matter how much pain it caused her. Gradually, she became increasingly uncomfortable with the inconsistency between her behavior (causing herself great pain by continuing to do all the household work) and the more rational idea -- that when one family member becomes impaired, it is reasonable to expect the others to contribute more.

When Carolyn's *cognitive dissonance* -- anxiety provoked by inconsistencies between belief and behavior -- had become sufficiently severe, her behavior changed. She began to consciously ignore her initial impulse to perform tasks she knew would then aggravate her pain and instead, deliberately forced herself to act assertively in her own best interests. Although she initially encountered some resistance when she began asking her husband and children to take over those household responsibilities that exacerbated her pain, "the genie was out of the bottle," and Carolyn could not comfortably return to the old pattern of behavior she had come to recognize as irrational and self-defeating. Although she continued to experience the impulse to do everything herself, her new pattern of assertive behavior eventually became predominant and she came to think of herself as a "reformed" super-homemaker.

Although it may be impossible to eradicate any and all self-prejudices, we can become aware of them and make a conscious decision to prevent them from controlling our behavior. And challenging our irrational self-prejudices with more reasonable views can be the first step in changing the way we act and feel. When we are able to consistently set aside our counterproductive self-prejudices, we can consider ourselves to be "reformed" or "in recovery."

Although we can't change who we are, we can alter what we do. By beginning to express ourselves and our feelings and insisting on equitable treatment, we can reform a tendency to passively permit others to take advantage of us. By beginning to listen carefully and take other people's wishes and feelings into consideration, we can reform a tendency to be self-preoccupied and inconsiderate. To consciously force ourselves to review the positive possibilities as well as the negative, we can become a "reformed" pessimist. By taking responsibility for our own experience and letting others be responsible for theirs, we can become a more "reformed" codependent. Although there are no "cures" and our initial impulses may never change, through conscious choice, we can prevent self-prejudices from sabotaging our experience.

The Hazards of Absolute Thinking

Some of us tend to see ourselves and the world in terms of absolutes: right or wrong, black or white, good or bad. Although this viewpoint can make life seem much less complicated, rarely do human affairs fall into such divergent categories. Judging human behavior, both our own and that of others, so categorically is unrealistic and can cause a great deal of unnecessary emotional stress. Thinking in absolute terms unreasonably implies that we are always capable of both knowing the best means to approach this particular problem and predicting the outcome of our actions. In real life, however, we're forced to make our decisions with very limited information and little ability to foresee the future. Even the "experts" rarely agree completely about anything. Sometimes exactly opposite courses of action each seem equally reasonable. Although it is inevitable that our decisions will sometimes appear, in retrospect, to have been unwise, at the time we made them, they almost certainly seemed to us to be for the best.

Decreasing the degree to which we think in absolute terms and expect ourselves or others to be perfect can then correspondingly diminish stress, anxiety and guilt. Terms such as "should," "must," "have to," "ought to," "need to," "supposed to," etc., imply an issue of morality (right vs. wrong) that simply does not apply to the vast majority of decisions that we make. Almost every course of action taken by either ourselves or others seemed, at the time, to be a good idea. Others may recommend alternative courses and our best sincere efforts will often fail, but our intent is almost always for the best.

When someone tells us what we "should" or "need to" do, or when we say these things to ourselves, what is usually meant is actually, "I think it might be a good idea to..." or "It might work out for the best if..." "You should..." usually means little more than "I recommend..." No one can predict the future or guarantee that any particular course of action will lead to the best possible outcome or the greatest peace of mind. The best we can do is to identify the course of action that seems to hold the greatest promise, given our current understanding of the circumstances.

Unfortunately even what may have seemed like great plans often go awry. For example, a career choice that seemed so perfect may suddenly become obsolete because of some unanticipated technological breakthrough. The place we choose to live may be unexpectedly struck by some natural or manmade disaster. Unforeseen illness or injury can rob us of our capacity to carry out our plans. Other people that we count on may disappoint us or become unavailable. There simply are no "sure things."

The uncertainty in life is demonstrated in the experiences of a seemingly wise person who inherited a substantial amount of money just before the turn of the nineteenth century. Being forward-thinking and wanting to expand his wealth, he invested his money in equal parts among the thirteen companies then producing automobiles in the United States. He had done a great deal of research and had become convinced that the automobile would soon become the standard mode of transportation. Unfortunately, a year later, Henry Ford started his company and put all of the thirteen automobile makers out of business. Although it is hard to find fault with the investor's logic and intent, the results of his actions were nevertheless quite disappointing.

Although each of us possesses a code of morality that draws a boundary between acceptable and unacceptable behavior, very few of the decisions we make actually involve an issue of morality. We are usually just trying to find the best path to follow. Absolute terms such as "should" inappropriately assign an issue of sin or stupidity to situations in which we are innocently trying to find the best course to navigate through the obstacles and challenges of our lives.

Absolute thinking implies that we deserve condemnation when our good faith choices fail to work out. By recognizing the irrationality of this proposition, we can avoid unwarranted and demoralizing guilt and self-belittlement.

Some people in positions of authority or celebrity make statements implying that anyone who fails to follow the course of action they recommended is "stupid" or a "loser." Although we all sometimes make choices that, in retrospect, seem unwise, no sincere and respectful person is ever a "loser," and no other person can know for certain what is best for us. It is an act of arrogance when another person attempts to tell us what we should believe or do.

Viewing the world in absolute terms leaves no room for other reasonable options that might prove equally or even more fruitful. With the exception of issues that involve our beliefs about morality, the concept of "should" rarely applies to the decisions that we make in life. The best that we can do is to take the course of action that seems most likely to succeed, with the understanding that events may not unfold as we hope, our mistakes are forgivable and we may decide to alter our plan at some point in the future.

The Human Comedy

A book called *The Human Comedy* by William Saroyan is one that can help us to put the events of our lives into a different perspective. Although life seems to present some of us with more than our share of trauma and loss, we all face the same challenge: coping with the difficulties we encounter, despite limited understanding and resources. The result is a world full of mistakes and mix-ups; a "human comedy."

In attempting to meet the demands and challenges of our lives, we are sometimes as inept as Laurel and Hardy moving a piano upstairs. If we can view the disappointing outcomes of our efforts and forgive the blunders of others as simply a natural part of the human comedy, we may be able to sometimes laugh and accept.

Although human technology has advanced in ways that sometimes seem miraculous, human beings have not. No matter how well-designed a human endeavor might be, once humans become actively involved the results are likely to be far from perfect. For example, although the Social Security Administration was established in order to provide benefits to prevent the elderly or disabled from becoming impoverished and homeless, such a large part of the agency's resources are now devoted to preventing non-qualified individuals from receiving benefits that applications from deserving and qualified individuals are often repeatedly rejected, with the result that some of us who have become occupationally disabled feel victimized all over again.

We are highly imperfect and vulnerable creatures, living in a world that is often incomprehensible and sometimes dangerous. By recognizing this fact and seeing those events of our lives that might demoralize us as simply part of the human comedy, we may occasionally be able to accept our difficulties with resigned humor rather than despair.

Comforting Thoughts about Disability

Here is a list of affirmations that may give comfort to those of us who have become occupationally disabled. Ideas such as these can be used to create rational alternatives to the counterproductive thoughts that can sometimes dominate our self-talk and damage our morale. Repeatedly rehearsing or even memorizing more constructive thoughts such as these can help us feel better and make progress in our efforts to cope and adjust.

1. For reasons we may not be able to understand, bad things often happen to good people. Although some people will be prejudiced against us as a result of our disability, our basic worth as an individual human is undiminished and we deserve no less respect than others.

2. If everything we have experienced were taken into consideration, our feelings would almost always be completely understandable, and they deserve to be respected.

3. Although losing our ability to work can magnify our normal self-doubts, it does not change who we are, the positive things we have accomplished, what we've learned, the loving relationships we've built, our achievements in the workplace and elsewhere, the kindness we have contributed to the world.

4. We possess a great gift in our power to act in the current

fleeting moment. No matter how many moments may have slipped by, each new moment brings us the opportunity to perceive our surroundings, take action and experience feelings. By investing our energy in here-and-now actions, and moving our thoughts away from past and future events we cannot control, we can replace feelings of helplessness with the satisfaction of knowing we controlled something.

5. By focusing our energy and attention on our current moment choices, we can manage any irrational and counter-productive tendencies to lament past disappointments and worry about what might come tomorrow.

6. Although we can't prevent others from acting selfishly and inconsiderately, we can attempt to model respect and thoughtfulness in our dealings with them.

7. Although becoming occupationally disabled can be a life changing event, we can prevent it from being a never ending crisis. By focusing our time and energy on those tasks that are within our control and letting go of the many frustrating aspects of life and disability that are outside our control, we can achieve greater peace of mind.

8. Although comparing ourselves to others in appearance, wealth, talent, capacity to work, etc. is completely normal, it is also a narcissistic concern that deserves the least consideration possible. Attaining peace of mind, developing our spirituality, growing intellectually and improving our loving relationships are more rewarding goals, and just as within our reach after becoming disabled as before.

9. At any point in time we can start a "new chapter" in our life story, let go of what has happened before, make a new plan of how to spend our time and energy, and then begin moving in a more positive direction.

10. By "turning over" and/or "letting go" of the distressing aspects of life that are beyond our control, we can reduce the feelings of helplessness that can sometimes immobilize us. By focusing as much energy as possible on those current moment tasks in which our actions may have some impact, we can increase our sense of competence.

11. Although American culture tends to value ownership and consumption, material wealth is never a requirement for (nor a guarantee of) personal development, loving relationships, peace of mind or feelings of self-fulfillment.

12. Each of us can improve ourselves by abandoning our demand for perfection and by becoming more accepting, tolerant and forgiving toward ourselves and others.

13. By recognizing all that we have already accomplished in our lives and the many obstacles that we had to overcome to do so, we can diminish feelings of hopelessness and increase our sense of self-respect.

14. Becoming disabled is not going to kill us and does not have to always seem like a complete catastrophe. We will recover when we can and survive what we have lost, as we always have before. Becoming disabled is just a big "bump in the road of life" that we will have to travel.

15. Most of us are temporarily knocked off balance when we become disabled and not at our best, which is why we deserve some special consideration and understanding. We will eventually adjust, grow stronger and regain our sense of self-confidence.

16. Every circumstance is temporary and every unpleasant moment passes. The future may bring us more pleasant experiences and there are always current steps that we can take to increase their probability.

17. Even though we have suffered a major loss we are still fortunate to live in a place and time that affords us many personal freedoms, relative safety and enough public assistance and/or opportunity to earn at least a subsistent living. Almost never do we have to suffer by going hungry or being without shelter.

18. All human beings have their many imperfections and weaknesses, and all of us feel overwhelmed at times by the traumas and losses that befall us. Despite it all, we can be successful by continuing to strive to improve ourselves and our quality of life.

19. When even close friends and family members fail to show understanding and compassion, it is usually an indication of their normal human limitations. The limitations of others do not reflect negatively upon us, although they may be a sign that it would be best to find others with whom to communicate about our disability.

20. Although it is normal to experience greater self-doubt and lowered self-esteem after becoming disabled, we can choose to view ourselves more rationally.   Disability is almost never deserved but is, instead, the result of inevitable human error and vulnerability in a world that is full of potential danger.

21.   By focusing our energy on those current moment choices over which we have some control; and by "turning over" and "letting go" of what we can't control, we can feel less helpless and have greater peace of mind.

22.   Even though we may have been an unfortunate victim of a disabling injury or illness, we still have the power to influence the quality of our own recovery, adjustment and future experience.

23.   As human beings, we can never be certain of what is for the best.   As unlikely as it may seem, becoming occupationally disabled may be the first difficult step in our path toward personal growth and maturity.

24.   Although we can't change the unreasonable judgments and opinions of others, we can learn to see them in a more rational perspective and be less affected by them.

25.   Rather than appearing to represent a sign of weakness or inadequacy, becoming disabled is often a reflection of admirable strengths, acts of conscientiousness, sincerity of the effort, industriousness and commitment to meet

responsibilities. Those of us who strive to do our best are at the greatest risk of sustaining a disabling injury or illness.

26. No matter how others may react, becoming disabled is not an indication of inferiority or inadequacy. Instead, it is a reflection of the fact that, like all human beings, we are physically and emotionally vulnerable and live in a dangerous world in which we are always at risk.

27. No matter how severe our physical impairment may be, we still have great potential for growth intellectually, emotionally, socially and spiritually.

28. Every crisis that we survive allows us to recognize that we are capable of surviving, and if we can muster sufficient patience and persistence, no crisis is insurmountable.

29. Others may do and say things that upset us, but they can't keep us upset if we refuse to replay their upsetting messages. By "letting go" of the negative things others say and do, making it their problem instead of ours, and by repeatedly rehearsing more rational alternative messages, we can improve the quality of our emotional experience.

30. As human beings, we are vulnerable but resilient. All of us have already overcome numerous obstacles in our lives, including that of surviving in a complicated and difficult world. Given time and support, each of us has the capacity to "bounce back" from adversity, even a disability.

31. There are always new, positive experiences to be had, wonderful movies that we haven't yet seen, great books we haven't yet read, caring and interesting people we haven't yet met, inspiring ideas and facts that await our discovery.

32. We can create new sources of positive life experience by identifying and then finding sufficient inspiration and courage to attempt the many rewarding activities that fall within the limitations of our disabilities.

33. By persistently taking action in the current day to explore new possibilities and "letting go" of those concerns over which we have no current day control, we can create the illusion of adaptability and gain greater respect from both ourselves and others.

34. By persistently striving to accomplish as much as we can, to accept what we can't accomplish, and to forgive ourselves for our limitations, we can enrich our lives and grow wiser as we age.

35. In this world of overwhelming challenges and stresses, we can function most effectively if we can use "psychological blinders" to block out the stresses we can't control and which might otherwise overwhelm and demoralize us.

36. Life goes on. Despite upsetting developments, we will most likely be able to live with what happens.

37. If we search enough, the "good" can be found in almost every person and circumstance.

38. Although we cannot be responsible for the actions of others, we can still be responsible for our own actions. If we strive to conform to rules of behavior that we respect (e.g., "Do unto others as you would have them do unto you"), we can seek peace of mind no matter how others might think or act.

39. By taking just one small, constructive step today, we can move forward on the pathway toward regaining our sense of purpose, self-confidence and hope. Surmounting the obstacles placed in our path by disability may seem as immense a challenge as eating an elephant, but both can be done, one bite at a time.

40. No one is perfect, but we will find many who will be reasonable and some who will be delightful.

41. Time changes everything. Our future almost always includes possibilities for love, creativity, self-sufficiency and greater peace of mind.

42. By attempting to make the most of each moment, we can create the most positive life experience possible.

43. By substituting more rational constructive ideas for the negative thoughts that underlie our emotional distress, we can increase our peace of mind. By listening more to what

others have to say and talking less about ourselves, we may become more understanding and improve our relationships.

44. There are more important things in life than being able to work, such as relationships with our loved ones, spiritual or philosophical development, intellectual growth, creative self-expression, etc.

45. Nothing that has happened in the past and no other person has the power to take away our future.

46. Making mistakes does not make us inadequate; it simply makes us human. There are no "right" and "wrong" ways of doing things, only those that we think might work better than others.

47. Being unable to meet our own expectations is not usually a sign of some inherent fault, but instead, reflects the fact that human behavior is controlled by many factors, only some of which are easily recognized or controlled by us.

48. Remember that the vulnerable child you once were still lives deep within each of us. Speak to him or her kindly and with encouragement by acknowledging positive attributes and overlooking human weaknesses.

49. Life is very complicated, often extremely difficult and sometimes simply brutal. We deserve to be forgiven for our mistakes and failures. In most cases, they were probably unavoidable.

50. By adopting new perspectives on our life events and circumstances, we can alter our attitude, mood, thoughts and behavior.

51. It may be important to change our set plans for life so that we can begin the different life that awaits us.

52. We can manage our anger by hesitating and thinking. By being patient in one moment of anger, we can escape many days of regret.

53. We almost always have enough to be happy if we're enjoying what we have and not worrying about what we don't have.

54. When we have important reasons to live (e.g., loved ones), we can bear any disability.

55. Even after becoming disabled, nothing is worth more than the current day. We can not relive yesterday, and tomorrow is still beyond our reach. We can make the most of this day.

56. In the face of a crisis, such as becoming disabled, we may find considerable support and helping resources: caring loved ones and family members, friends, medical personnel, legal representatives, therapists, etc., all of whom may be called upon to help us adjust and survive.

57. By reminding ourselves of the good fortune and the

resources that we still possess even after becoming disabled, we may be able to find a constructive outlook that will keep helplessness to a minimum and allow us to make the most of our remaining opportunities.

58. Medical science has now proven what we have all known for decades: Ineffectual anger, that which leads to no constructive action, damages our health and shortens our lives. We can make our anger constructive by converting it into energy that motivates us to take positive action.

59. Aggressive or destructive action damages both the target and the perpetrator. We can make the world a better place in which to live (for ourselves, those we care about and others) when we resist the temptation to lash out.

60. Serene acceptance allows us the best chance of solving the problems life puts before us, and also promotes our physical and emotional well-being. While it may be easier to be despondent or to hate, it is much healthier to accept and love.

61. Attitude may be more important than education, money, circumstances, appearance, giftedness or skill. We make choices every day, regarding the attitude we will embrace for that day. Although we cannot change most of what happens in life, our experiences are based more on how we react to those events than on the events themselves.

62. By being aware of "the dirty little tricks" that our

minds can play on us: magnifying minor or temporary problems into catastrophes, confusing what we can and can't control, damning ourselves for making ordinary human mistakes, etc., we can avoid falling into the trap of negative thinking that can block us from taking constructive action.

63. Many of us have been taught as children that it is important to be perfect, and that we have to be better, richer, prettier and more successful than our peers. By recognizing the fallacy of these ideas and accepting imperfection in ourselves and others, we can increase peace of mind.

64. It may be possible to accept the distressing events of our lives more serenely by attempting to imagine how someone we greatly respect might have responded. How would Gandhi, Mother Theresa, Christ, Buddha, Mohammed, Abraham, Martin Luther King, Jr. or Eleanor Roosevelt have felt and acted?

65. Even after becoming disabled life can be an opportunity to explore, test and experience what we never knew before and sometimes even what we never knew was possible.

66. Neither having the physical capacity to work nor being physically unimpaired is a prerequisite to having "peak experiences," those that cause us to feel closely in touch with a higher power.

67. Disability is a relative concept. Almost every one of us

is physically impaired in some way. It is most difficult to adjust to occupational disability when we have lost capacities that we once had. We adjusted long ago to those capacities we never had.

68. The richest and most rewarding lives can be those that are forged out of winning a messy battle with adversity. We may wish that adversity never strikes, yet if we persist in our efforts to adjust, we can be made stronger by it.

69. For all of our faults and weaknesses, human beings also possess the built-in capacity to survive difficult circumstances and emerge stronger than before. Surviving a crisis such as becoming occupationally disabled can ultimately be a positive, life-changing experience.

70. We have the potential to rebound from virtually every life crisis and thrive afterward. We are never required to remain hopeless or helpless. What doesn't kill us can make us stronger.

71. Our greatest heroes are often those who have been tested by severe adversity, survived and demonstrated courage and persistence in doing so. It may in fact be that only by experiencing pain, distress and confusion that we can fully appreciate the positive aspects of life such as joy and contentment.

72. Contending with the shock of becoming disabled and eventually finding a new purpose and meaning in life can

bring us a greater sense of satisfaction than we might have ever known in a tranquil, carefree existence. Sometimes we must *hurt* in order to *grow*.

73. Becoming disabled can change us for the better. It can result in greater compassion, insight, altruism, creativity and more appreciation of our blessings. Becoming disabled can help us see more clearly what is truly important in life.

74. It is normal to feel dazed and anxious when we become disabled. But if we persist in reorienting our lives around what we determine to be the most important elements of life that remain within our reach, our lives can become richer and more gratifying than ever.

75. By choosing our response to becoming disabled, we can either become mired in depression and despair or we can tackle the challenges of reorienting our lives and making them more meaningful than before.

76. By tapping into our unrecognized capacities to survive and adjust, we can surprise ourselves with our own strength.

77. If we devote ourselves to the task, each of us can carve out a rewarding life, even within the limitations and the difficulties created by our disability.

78. By introducing ourselves to a different perspective on our lives and disabilities, one that challenges irrational ideas and makes us feel more hopeful, we will probably be able to

accomplish more, see ourselves in a more favorable light and better improve the quality of our life experience.

79. Becoming disabled does not diminish our capacity to act honorably, to show respect for others and ourselves, to treat others as equals, to be considerate and to be honest. If we make honor the most important consideration in our lives (above wealth, popularity, etc.), then our lost ability to work is a crisis overcome rather than a catastrophe.

VI

Shifting Into Gear

Like all major life crises, becoming disabled can initially cause even the strongest of us to become so discouraged and anxious that we may find it difficult to take decisive action toward re-establishing our sense of hope, self-confidence and purpose. The biggest obstacle to conquering disability is often just *getting started.*

The goal of this chapter is to assist in identifying manageable constructive steps that can start us on the path toward recovery and adjustment, as well as to help generate sufficient energy and motivation to begin taking those steps. Although we can be comforted by the knowledge that our feelings are completely understandable and by the fact that many others have successfully adjusted to disability, it takes understanding-based *action* for us to regain control over our experience of life.

By following the next steps presented, we can set in motion an upward spiral of small, constructive actions that can help us reclaim a sense of meaning and purpose. By recognizing that we still have opportunities, finding inspiration to pursue them, setting reasonable goals and eliminating the roadblocks that can deter us, we can construct a program for success.

Finding Reasons to Believe

We almost never attempt what we believe to be impossible. It makes no sense to strive for something we are convinced is beyond our reach. One of the first problems we face in attempting to recover from the trauma of disabling injury or illness is recognizing that we are almost never beyond hope, that even in our lowest moments we still have the capacity to improve our life experience through our own efforts.

Even when disability has caused us to become preoccupied with losses and fears, each of us continues to possess the capacity to create a successful life experience. There are always ways that we can strive to improve ourselves and our relations with others. No matter how incapacitated we are, we still retain the ability to develop ourselves intellectually, philosophically, spiritually and/or interpersonally. If we choose, we can make it our goal to become better informed, more self-expressive, more creative, wiser, more understanding, more closely connected to God (or whatever our conception of a higher power might be), more involved in a cause we believe to be important, more grateful, more forgiving of ourselves and others and/or more strongly bonded to those we love. If we can limit our preoccupation with what we've lost and focus as much attention and energy as possible on what we still have, we can accept ownership of our disability and assume responsibility for finding the "tools" that will allow us to manage the challenges that accompany our disability.

With determination and persistence each of us is capable of learning to focus our energy on our current moment choices, the only means we have of exercising power and gradually regaining a sense of control over our own experience. We can adopt a more rational perspective on life that will help us manage the distressing thoughts and feelings that can impede our efforts to recover and adjust. We can find new activities and involvements that will make our lives rewarding and enhance our sense of usefulness. We can improve our ability to speak up and express our wishes, and in doing so, have greater control and increase our self-respect. Perhaps most importantly, we can make more of our personal relationships and develop stronger feelings of being connected to something greater than ourselves. We can begin to show greater respect for our bodies and achieve a greater sense of physical and emotional well-being. And by taking these steps, we can create a far more rewarding life experience, thus *winning the disability challenge.*

<u>Building New Life Connections</u>

An examination of how we are "connected" to the world around us can help us to not only appreciate how disability has altered our lives, but also why it may have caused us to feel so disconnected. Even more importantly, it can help us begin the process of selecting and pursuing new connections. The "Life Connection Circle" presented in Exercise 3 was created by Jack, a career plumber who had become disabled by a combination of back and knee injuries. He was referred for a mental health consultation when his orthopedic surgeon noticed that he had also become quite depressed.

As can be seen from his "Life Connection Circle", before he became disabled Jack had been an active person. In addition to his work, Jack was connected to life through his marriage, his children, his dog, weekly poker games with an old group of friends, watching movies and automotive sports, playing golf and racquetball, a significant involvement in his church and faith, and regular visits with his sister. Creating this "Life Connection Circle" helped Jack see how his disability had altered his overall life experience and how it had suddenly deprived him of some major aspects of his life that helped him feel grounded in the world around him. Not only had Jack lost his capacity to work, a major anchor in life (as it is for most of us), but he had lost his ability to enjoy playing racquetball, golf and even some aspects of his relationships with his wife and children. It was not surprising that Jack felt as if a large piece of his world was torn away, leaving him disconnected and distressed.

Exercise #3: The Life Connection Circle

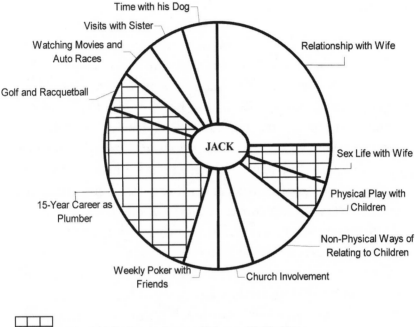

= Former activity/ involvement no longer possible because of disabling injury

In addition to helping him better understand the emotional impact of his disability, drawing his Life Connection Circle also helped Jack to feel grateful for those life connections that remained intact and identified potential ways of strengthening his feeling of being connected. Simply recognizing the possibility that the void in his life created by his disability might be fulfilled increased Jack's optimism and diminished his sense of helplessness. The exercise led him to set goals for improving and expanding his relationships with others (particularly his children) and introduced him to new activities and interests (becoming a volunteer driver for the senior center near his home and joining an additional poker group) that may help him feel more connected.

In order to construct our own Life Connections Circle, we start by making a list of all the people and activities to which we usually devote time in any given month. We begin with the people and activities involved in our daily lives, such as our spouse or life partner, children, parents, grandchildren, work, hobbies, close friends or relatives, recreational activities, religious and/or community involvements and pets. Then we add those people and activities that are involved in our life only intermittently or occasionally, such as other relatives and friends and other sources of entertainment. Then we divide the top half of the circle between those two items on our list that are of greatest importance to us, giving the greatest space to the most important connection.

Then we divide the bottom half of the circle into spaces representing the remaining items on our list, we devote greater space to those that are more important to us and less space to those of less importance. Then we re-draw our Life Connection Circle and make adjustments in the spaces allotted to each of our various life connections as we find to be appropriate based upon their relative importance in our life. Finally, we identify each connection that was totally or partially lost as the result of our disability and we shade that area of the circle. This experience can improve our understanding of how disability has impacted our life, stimulate ideas for strengthening connections that remain intact and point us in the direction of new involvements that might replace those that have been lost.

<u>Inspiring Ourselves Into Action</u>

In addition to helping us appreciate the impact of disability, creating a Life Connection Circle can lead us to see that our lives are still important even after we become disabled and can provide us with sources of inspiration. Even at our lowest point, we can be inspired by our feelings about our children, a loving spouse or partner, our parents, a close friend or relative, a religious faith or conviction, a creative goal, a cherished recreational activity or a political or social cause that we feel strongly about. Our concern for the welfare of our loved ones can sometimes inspire us to do our best for their sake and to take constructive action in order to show them how we would want them to respond if they were struck by a major life crisis.

Sometimes, we can find inspiration in our own histories. Each of our lives has in many ways already been a success story and some have been remarkable. Before we became occupationally disabled, we had to first prove our capacity to work, to present ourselves in a manner that led someone to select us for employment and to demonstrate the capacity to consistently adapt to a work setting and manage work responsibilities. Before those successes, each of us had to first survive our own childhood and the family structure that we grew up within, many of which were quite possibly less than ideal and all of which were full of problems. We somehow successfully coped with the considerable pressures of adolescence. One way or another we managed to obtain an education and some work skills by successfully avoiding the numerous pitfalls that derail so many lives (e.g., alcohol or drug addiction, street violence, criminal activity or victimization, breaking down under the many pressures of life, etc.).

Most of us have many other accomplishments as well. Many of us have succeeded as parents and/or mates (sometimes despite not having any good role model). Some of us have become skilled in crafts, music or sports. Some of us have become successful in community or faith-based activities, while some of us succeeded academically and/or vocationally. If we managed to accomplish those successes, despite those obstacles, we can overcome the obstacle of disability and find success again.

Our past history of accomplishments and overcoming many obstacles can sometimes be used as a source of self-inspiration. Reviewing lists of both our life accomplishments and the life obstacles we overcame to achieve those successes can create a sense of resiliency that we may not have felt before. For example, one client was able to recognize that before becoming disabled she had managed to graduate from high school, move to a different state on her own, secure a highly responsible public service position, work successfully in that position for twenty years and raise a very successful and loving daughter, all despite the fact that she grew up in an impoverished family of eleven children.

She was repeatedly told by her father that she was "good for nothing." Yet she was able to see that she demonstrated great resiliency in the past and this recognition boosted her fractured self-confidence and provided some inspiration in her efforts to overcome the challenges of her disability.

We can also take inspiration from the stories of others who have overcome even more severe disabilities than ours to lead actively fulfilling lives and make contributions of worldwide impact. Public figures such as Christopher Reeve and Stephen Hawking, both who have overcome seemingly catastrophic disabilities, can help us see that each of us is capable of creating a crucial life despite our disabilities.

Hanging On to What We've Got

Self-sufficient functioning is a primary goal of virtually all recovery programs. Three factors often determine the level of recovery we are able to attain:

1. *Rehabilitation:* The restoring of as many lost capacities as possible (e.g., reconditioning our bodies in physical therapy)

2. *Compensation:* Developing alternative ways of functioning (e.g., replacing running with a low-trauma exercise such as swimming or studying computer operation in order to replace lost capacity to perform construction work, etc.)

3. *Retention:* Doing all we can to continue performing as many of our usual everyday activities as possible (continuing

to be as active as possible within our medical restrictions, staying in touch with the important people in our lives, continuing to exercise in a manner that is within our own limitations, etc.)

This third factor, retention, is often overlooked but can be of vital importance to our recovery and adjustment. It is entirely normal to be afraid of pain and/or further injury after becoming disabled. It is also best, however, for us to maintain as much independent functioning and as many of our normal routines as is reasonably possible given our medical limitations. For example, some of us who have been driving our entire adult lives become so insecure after becoming disabled that we don't start driving again, even when no longer prevented by physical limitations.

Many of us who become disabled withdraw from our usual patterns of social interaction. Although we often find it appropriate to minimize contact with those of our friends and family members who prove insensitive to our difficulties, staying connected with a social support network can keep our morale up and help us to see that successful adjustment is possible. Becoming connected with other disabled workers, who are likely to have personal understanding of the challenges we're facing, can be of particular benefit. By maintaining our connections with others and retaining as much self-sufficiency as possible, we can speed our own recovery and adjustment.

We can also make a difference in our recovery by becoming active participants in our own medical care. Our own actions are likely to contribute more to our recovery and adjustment than anything that any other person (including our doctors) can do for us. There are frequent limits to how much medical treatment can help us. In many cases, our medical care consists principally of managing symptoms (such as pain), while the natural healing forces of our bodies do their work. Although medications can help to control symptoms, almost all have the potential to cause unwanted side effects or adverse reactions. Whereas surgeries are usually beneficial, they involve additional trauma to the body. Occasionally, they fail completely and even when "successful", they rarely restore full pre-injury functioning. It is often our commitment to post-surgical physical therapy and self-care efforts that plays the major role in our long-term surgical outcome.

We can then improve our own medical prognosis by attempting to become what Dr. Bernie Siegel refers to as "an exceptional patient"; one who takes an active role in developing and then following through on the treatment plan, demands respect and appropriate assistance, refuses to passively accept that a positive outcome is impossible, and persists in searching for the best medical care available and the self-help tools and techniques that will permit the most effective possible life adjustment.

Listing Goals and Scheduling for Success

Creating a list of goals and keeping a daily schedule are two simple and straightforward ways that we can begin moving in a positive direction. By having a plan for each day, including several items from our list of goals, we can attempt to reestablish the sense of organization that, in many cases, had previously been imposed by our work. To the extent that we are able to complete any of our scheduled goal activities, we may be able to experience a sense of accomplishment and prove that we are not powerless. Finally, we can strive for greater peace of mind by forgiving ourselves for whatever scheduled goals we fail to accomplish in the current day and transferring them to our schedule for tomorrow (or back to our master list of goals so that they can be included on some other day's schedule). And as we perform these actions, we can prepare to make the most of both the current moment and those to come in the future.

We can begin by constructing *a list of goals and activities*, including every positive goal or potentially constructive activity we can identify. We can start by listing those actions that might improve our sense of financial or physical well-being, such as obtaining, completing and submitting applications for any disability benefit not already claimed. Next, add every action we can conceive of that might reduce our living expenses (e.g., selling a car, looking for a less expensive residence, etc.). Also, list steps to explore opportunities for alternative careers, legal or medical consultations we may want to pursue and actions that might improve our health or comfort. List ways of showing our loved ones how we feel about them, as well as any activities that we've abandoned, but reasonably hope to resume in the future.

List everything we might ever want to do. Every time we think or hear of some action that might be productive in some way, might be enjoyable, improve our experience or advance us towards a goal *we can write it down on our list.* When someone recommends a television show, movie, play, musical recording, church service, book, trip or some other entertainment or inspiration, we can add it to our list. Each time we pass an interesting store, library, museum or park, we can add it to our list. When we think of some action that might please someone whose feelings are important to us, we can add it to our list. When we hear of an opportunity for involvement that sounds like it might be of interest at a church, hospital, senior center, charity, political or social action group, we can add it to our list. Every time we think of some personal or family task that might benefit from our attention, we can add it to our list.

Our list of possibilities does not have to be long to be useful, but it cannot be too long. *We are not obligated to complete every potential goal and action we list but each remains an option, a documented possibility.* Even if we never attempt any of the items on our list, simply observing that numerous possibilities exist is likely to reduce our feelings of helplessness, boost our morale and enhance our motivation. Here is a list of goals and activities that we might include:

1.   Listen to a new music CD
2.   Watch a TV program recommended by a friend
3.   Read something inspirational
4.   Attend a religious service or church function
5.   Begin a jigsaw puzzle that is not too difficult
6.   Plant something
7.   Work in the garden
8.   Draw a picture
9.   Make a collage
10.   Write a letter to someone else or to yourself
11.   Take a walk

12. Engage in exercise within your physical limitations
13. Review your list of "blessings"
14. Seek information about disability benefits online
15. Request course catalogs from the local community college, adult school or city recreation department
16. Visit the library
17. Check out and listen to a book on tape or CD
18. Volunteer at a school, hospital, library, charity, senior center, etc.
19. Visit a point of interest, such as a museum, park, beach, bookstore, college, lake, forest, etc.
20. Work on a hobby (e.g., putting together a model, sorting a collection, sewing, photography, etc.)
21. Look for a pet (or if you have one, play with them)
22. Make an appointment to see an attorney or doctor
23. Call an old friend

When making our "List of Goals and Activities," it'd be best to try and include activities that involve physical exercise, mental challenges, self-enrichment, self-expression and contributions to the welfare of others in our community. In the absence of exercise, both our bodies and our minds deteriorate. Expressing ourselves through artistic endeavors and constructive hobbies can occupy our thoughts and lend a sense of accomplishment. Developing an intellectual and spiritual understanding can enhance our sense of well-being and peace of mind. Contributing to the community and/or helping others can make us aware that we still have reason to be thankful, briefly distract our thoughts from our own problems, and provide a sense of having contributed something positive to the world. Although our attention is often irresistibly drawn to what we have lost, with concerted effort we can shift our focus to taking advantage of the multitude of possibilities and opportunities that remain available to us.

After compiling our list of goals and activities, the next step towards a better structuring of our time is to begin completing a schedule for each day, such as that depicted in Illustration A. Because it can serve as a calendar and a daily schedule, either an appointment book for the current year or an electronic notebook is ideal for this task. Neither is essential, however. As long as we have some way of calendaring appointments and special occasions (such as a monthly wall calendar), and a daily schedule to which items from our goals and activities list can be transferred, we can begin imposing a greater sense of order and control over our lives. Scheduling can include: appointments with doctors, lawyers, therapists, court dates, public agencies, meetings with friends or family members, haircut appointments or church group meetings, etc. In addition, we can record the birthdays of people we want to remember as well as any and all events that we might want to attend.

ILLUSTRATION A

MY DAILY SCHEDULE FOR   Thursday,   06/22/06
                          (day of week) (mm/dd/yy)

Time	Activity
7:00 a.m.	20-minute walk
7:30 a.m.	Shower, dress
8:00 a.m.	Drive kids to school
8:30 a.m.	Breakfast, take medications, inspirational reading
9:00 a.m.	Call friend or relative
9:30 a.m.	
10:00 a.m.	Physical therapy appointment
10:30 a.m.	
11:00 a.m.	Check out health clubs nearest home
11:30 a.m.	
12:00 p.m.	Lunch with friend or relative
12:30 p.m.	
1:00 p.m.	Pharmacy
1:30 p.m.	Dry cleaner
2:00 p.m.	Appointment with Dr.
2:30 p.m.	
3:00 p.m.	Inquire about courses offered at Community College
3:30 p.m.	
4:00 p.m.	Household responsibilities
4:30 p.m.	
5:00 p.m.	Household responsibilities
5:30 p.m.	
6:00 p.m.	Dinner
6:30 p.m.	
7:00 p.m.	20-minute walk
7:30 p.m.	
8:00 p.m.	Favorite television
8:30 p.m.	
9:00 p.m.	Complete schedule for tomorrow
9:30 p.m.	Read novel or work puzzle
10:00 p.m.	Take medications
10:30 p.m.	
11:00 p.m.	Bed
11:30 p.m.	Relaxation exercises

Illustration B, located on the following page, presents a blank schedule that can be copied for use on a daily basis. Whether using a page from an appointment book, an electronic notebook or a copied daily schedule, we can complete a new schedule each evening for the following day. First we schedule previously-made commitments, and/or appointments and our routine daily activities (e.g., meals, showering, taking medications, etc.). Then we can fill in open time with items from our list of goals and activities.

Once our daily schedule has been completed, our next challenge is to see what we can accomplish during that particular day. Events rarely unfold exactly as we anticipate or wish and we may find that we have planned more than we can reasonably accomplish. Sometimes, we may fail to adequately provide time for rest or relaxation, or our plans are interrupted by unforeseen events. No matter how the day's events may transpire, however, the goal at the end of each day is to accept what occurred, place as much value on what we were able to accomplish as possible, and excuse ourselves for failing to accomplish the rest. After taking as much pleasure as possible in any constructive activity we were able to carry out, we can then begin construction of a schedule for the next day. In doing so, we can consider transferring those items from today's schedule that we did not manage to complete. Or, we can return them to our master list of goals and activities so that they can be reconsidered for inclusion on the schedule of the subsequent day.

ILLUSTRATION B

MY DAILY SCHEDULE FOR _____, _____
                                   (day of week)   (mm/dd/yy)

7:00a.m. _____

7:30a.m. _____

8.00 a.m. _____

8:30 a.m. _____

9:00 a.m. _____

9:30 a.m. _____

10:00 a.m._____

10:30 a.m._____

11:00 a.m._____

11:30 a.m._____

12:00 p.m._____

12:30 p.m._____

1:00 p.m._____

1:30 p.m._____

2:00 p.m._____

2:30 p.m._____

3:00 p.m._____

3:30 p.m._____

4:00 p.m._____

4:30 p.m._____

5:00 p.m._____

5:30 p.m._____

6:00 p.m._____

6:30 p.m._____

7:00 p.m._____

7:30 p.m._____

8:00 p.m._____

8:30 p.m._____

9:00 p.m._____

9:30 p.m._____

10:00 p.m._____

10:30 p.m._____

11:00 p.m._____

11:30 p.m._____

Forgive Us For Our Failures

Failure is an inevitable aspect of almost every successful human endeavor. Most meaningful accomplishments depend upon our ability to cope with feelings of having failed, without becoming so discouraged that we give up. If we can view our "failures" as signals to alter our direction, rather than as signs that we should abandon our efforts, we will have the greatest possible chance of ultimate success.

Simply refusing to give up may perhaps be the most important prerequisite for success. A study of self-made multimillionaires found that the only way in which they were different than less financially successful individuals of equal ability and education was that they were not deterred by repeated failures. Despite many failed endeavors, they continued to seek their fortune, whereas others responded to failure by settling for security and abandoning hopes of great wealth.

Our goal is to make each "failure" as acceptable and forgivable as possible so that we can move ahead to success. If we can forgive ourselves for each misstep and simply persist in the face of every perceived setback, we will eventually be successful despite our disability.

Failures are inevitable. We have limited understanding of the forces that shape events or sometimes even our own behavior. We are also very poor at predicting the future. Even what might seem the wisest of plans today frequently unravels tomorrow. Each of our attempts at constructive action is an experiment. We can set goals and make plans, but we are unlikely to be able to fulfill all of these as we hoped. When the outcome of our efforts is disappointing, our challenge is to learn from the experience, "let go" of what occurred (and can't be changed) and revise our plan.

Many of us experience anger at ourselves when we fail to take steps that we believe to be necessary ("must," "have to," "need to") or proper ("should," "ought to," "supposed to"). We ask ourselves, "What's wrong with me? Why do I procrastinate?" The answer is that this type of behavior is completely normal. Our actions are controlled by complex laws of human behavior that are often difficult to understand. Like the behavior of a ball on a pool table or a car on an icy road, the course of action we take in our daily lives is determined by the interaction of many factors. Our belief about what is proper or necessary is just one of those factors and it alone is often not strong enough to either initiate or sustain action. Our behavior is ultimately determined by a complex interaction between motivation, capacity, difficulty and resistance. The course of action that we take is that which has the strongest combined force pressing in its direction.

We are always "doing" something, even if it might only be lying in a bed. We are engaged in that activity because the combined forces pressing us toward that behavior outweigh the combined forces pressing us to perform any other behavior. It makes no sense to get angry at ourselves when we fail to follow a particular course of action. This would be equivalent to getting angry at our car when its wheels spin in the snow rather than moving the car forward. Just as the solution to the spinning car wheels is to alter the dynamics of the situation by improving traction, the solution to our behavioral problems is to alter the motivational factors involved so that the total force pressing toward the desired action is predominant.

A client reported being "disgusted" with himself because he had failed to remove his possessions from a rented storage space he could no longer afford. As a hard-working and obsessive-compulsive individual who had sustained a chronically disabling lumbar spine injury, he could not understand his failure and was angry with himself for incurring additional charges he had hoped to avoid. An exploration of the factors that might have been creating resistance helped him recognize that while he wanted to avoid paying the additional storage charges, he wanted even more to avoid the exacerbated back pain he anticipated would result from the effort of moving his belongings. By enlisting the help of his adult son, he was able to sufficiently alter the forces at work so that he was able to both confront and accomplish the task.

Whenever we succeed in changing a pattern of behavior, it means that we have somehow altered the forces affecting us in such a way that the total press to perform the new behavior has become stronger than the total press to perform the former behavior. This is what occurs when an alcoholic succeeds in becoming sober through the Alcoholics Anonymous (AA) program. Almost every alcoholic recognizes the great importance of drinking less. Unfortunately, this recognition alone usually proves insufficient to produce extended sobriety. For many individuals, the AA Twelve Step program somehow alters the behavioral forces at play and increases the ability of those individuals to refrain from consuming alcoholic beverages.

The reason we sometimes fail to follow the course of action that seems preferable or logical usually falls within one or more of these categories:

1. We lack sufficient motivation
2. We believe that we are too incapacitated to reasonably expect to be successful
3. The anticipated payoff ("reinforcement") for completing the activity is insufficient
4. Competing motivations toward alternate actions (e.g., eating a sandwich, watching a television show, calling a friend, or playing a video game) are stronger
5. The resistance is too great (e.g., fear of aggravating injury, fear of failure, fear that someone of importance might not approve, some part of the activity is distasteful, etc.)

We may be able to change our behavior by adjusting these factors. But our actions would always make perfect sense if we understood all of the factors at play. Although the complexity of human behavior makes this type of understanding virtually impossible, recognizing the fact may help us forgive ourselves.

If we can forgive ourselves when we fail to accomplish goals, we will feel better and will probably be more able to tackle those goals on another day. If we continue to find ourselves unable to complete an action even after repeated attempts, that goal may represent an unreasonable expectation. If lack of energy or emotional control seems to be preventing us from being able to accomplish our goals, it may be time to consider consulting our personal physician or a mental health specialist.

Neither recovery from emotional trauma nor adjustment to major loss is likely to take place in a straight-line fashion. Instead, every period of progress is likely to be followed by a setback, a brief episode of exacerbated symptoms during which it seems that no progress has been made at all and we can easily come to feel overwhelmed and helpless. We can survive these episodes by keeping in mind the fact that almost all human progress occurs in a sporadic manner, and that intermittent setbacks are almost invariably part of the recovery process. Our feelings of failure during these times represent only a temporary illusion. If we can reject these self-defeating thoughts, or "turn them over" to a higher power, we can prevent them from derailing our recovery efforts and continue to strive for progress.

Because we are fallible human beings we often "fall off the wagon." As long as we climb back on board each time we fall, however, we will eventually succeed. One of life's greatest blessings is that each morning we have the golden opportunity to start anew, to try to set aside what has gone before, forgive ourselves and others for past failures and attempt to seize this day by getting as much from it as we possibly can.

VII

The Power of Self-Expression

If we can express our wishes and feelings openly and honestly we will increase the likelihood that they will be respected. This type of self-assertion can also change how we are viewed by others, and perhaps even more importantly, how we view ourselves. As we adjust to becoming disabled and find ourselves facing pressure from doctors, attorneys, claims administrators, social services personnel, and even friends and family who may not know how to best respond, the ability to effectively communicate what we want is more important than ever. Through self-assertion we can establish that we are not helpless, protect our feelings and rights from being overlooked, and make the most of our relationships with others.

<u>Our Perfect Right</u>

"Everyone has the right to freedom of opinion and expression.
To seek, receive, and impart information and ideas."
Article XIX, UN Universal Declaration of Human Rights
(As drafted by Eleanor Roosevelt)

To psychologists, assertiveness is the ability to express ourselves honestly by clearly stating what we want or believe, without showing disrespect for others. It means standing up for our personal rights and expressing our thoughts, feelings and beliefs in direct and appropriate ways that do not violate any other person's rights or feelings. The basic messages of assertiveness are:

This is what I think.

This is what I feel.

This is how I see the situation.

This is my preference.

This is what I want.

--all expressed without any attempt to intimidate, humiliate or degrade anyone else.

Neither aggressiveness nor passivity tends to represent responsible, assertive behavior. Passivity involves violating our own rights by failing to express our honest feelings and thoughts, making it easy for others to disregard them. The messages of passivity are:

I don't count.

My feelings don't matter.

My thoughts aren't important.

You can take advantage of me.

Aggression, on the other hand, involves the expression of thoughts and feelings in a way that somehow harms or disrespects someone else. The messages of aggression are:

This is what I think and you're stupid for believing differently.

This is what I want and what you want doesn't matter.

This is what I feel and your feelings don't count.

Aggressiveness and passivity are typically viewed as the endpoints on a continuum of characteristic response styles, with assertiveness falling in the middle. Whereas assertiveness usually involves making "I" statements that communicate an internal state of the speaker ("I want...," "I feel..."), aggressiveness typically involves making "you" statements that blame ("You did...") or insult ("You're a..."). Passivity, on the other hand, usually involves making no response at all or making one that is so weak that it is easily disregarded by others.

Passive compliance may avoid conflicts but it also tends to reduce the frequency with which we obtain goals, often resulting in others taking advantage of us and generally leading to frustration, feelings of incompetence, increased fear of interacting with others and diminished respect not only by others, but by ourselves as well. Although it may often be easiest to "go along to get along," it is rarely a strategy that turns out for the best in the long run.

Aggressiveness tends to result in anger, dislike and avoidance by others. No one likes a bully and that's how aggressive people are usually viewed. Even when aggression leads to success in obtaining goals, the cost in terms of personal relationships can be steep. Assertiveness, on the other hand, tends to give us the best chance to obtain our goals while at the same time increasing respect from others and for ourselves. Even when being assertive does not produce results, we still gain some measure of self-respect in knowing that we have expressed our wish while, at the same time, respecting the feelings of others.

Self-Assertion for Self-Respect

Even though others will often exercise their right to decline, asking for what we want both improves the probability that we will get it (or at least an acceptable compromise) and enhances our sense of power over our lives. Even more importantly, however, the assertive expression of our wishes honors our feelings and implies that we are worthy of consideration. Self-assertion provides us an opportunity to improve our image in our own eyes, as well as those of others.

As children, we had little control over the amount of respect we were shown. We assumed that the manner in which we were treated by the most important people in our lives accurately reflected our worth. As adults, however, we have the power to alter our view of ourselves in the same way that our opinions of others are shaped: We watch behavior and make judgments.

When we witness passive acceptance of unreasonable treatment or circumstances, whether by ourselves or others, a degree of respect is lost. On the other hand, when we observe responsible, assertive action, like making wishes known without showing disrespect, our esteem is slightly enhanced. Our assertive responses defy our subconscious notion that we may be less deserving or adequate than others.

Who are the people we most respect? Would any of them passively allow their feelings to be disregarded? Probably not. Would they speak up to call attention to their preferences? Almost certainly. Even when we don't get exactly what we want, our feelings and relationships will almost always be better in the long run if we ask that others respect our personal boundaries, limitations, feelings and preferences, while simultaneously showing respect for theirs.

Sometimes it can be helpful to select a model, someone for whom we have great respect and wish to emulate. When I encounter difficulty or conflict, I try to ask myself, "What would Gandhi do?" This thought has helped me both stay calm and search for a response that would be reasonable, assertive and compassionate. Other heroes who can be looked to as models of responsible assertiveness include spiritual visionaries (e.g., Buddha, Christ, Mohammed, Abraham, etc.), political or military figures (e.g., George Washington, Thomas Jefferson, Abraham Lincoln, Theodore Roosevelt, Rosa Parks, John F. Kennedy,

"You're really a great teacher. I'm so glad I took your class."

More complicated situations can call for empathic assertions, a response that is designed to disarm aggressiveness and alter a potential conflict situation into one of mutual exploration for compromise and resolution. Empathic assertions typically consist of three parts:

(1) An empathy statement acknowledging the other person's rights and feelings;

(2) A conflict statement expressing our reasons for wanting a change; and

(3) An action statement explaining precisely what we would like to occur or what we intend to do.

Examples would be:

(1) "I know that you're under a lot of pressure...

(2) ...but I can't submit my proposal without your approval...

(3) ...so please let me know when you'll be able to review it."

or

(1) "I know that it's difficult to get around without a car...

(2) ...but I've made plans for this evening...

(3) ...so I won't be able to loan you my car or drive you tonight."

When dealing with sensitive people or sensitive issues, adding the empathic statement could improve the effect of an assertive response by conveying recognition of the other person's difficult situation or feelings, before addressing the issues of conflict and rights. This approach is particularly useful when we are concerned that we may be perceived as overly demanding. The empathic statement can indeed help prepare the listener to be more "open" to our subsequent message. Furthermore, the act of conceiving an empathic statement might actually help us to better understand the other person's viewpoint and increase the probability of reaching a workable compromise.

Nonverbal Assertiveness

There is more to being assertive than just *what* we say. *How* we say it, the volume and tone of our voice, our facial expressions, body posture, gestures, eye contact and inter-personal distance can be equally vital to getting our message across. By making our nonverbal behavior consistent with our assertive verbal message, we add strength, support and emphasis to the content of our message. What we say is most likely to be perceived as assertive if our voice is appro-priately loud to the situation, our eye contact is frequent but not intense, we stand straight at an appropriate distance, and we speak fluently and clearly. For those of us who are easygoing and accommodating by nature, becoming more assertive may involve breaking new ground. If we find it difficult to maintain direct eye contact, we can look at the forehead or chin of the person being addressed or simply make very brief eye contact at regular intervals. When we have difficulty expressing our message without awkward hesitation, *repeated rehearsal* can improve our statements and delivery. Sometimes it can be helpful to think of ourselves as actors playing a role. By rehearsing our assertive lines until we are able to deliver them convincingly, we can create an illusion of self-confidence that may eventually fool even ourselves. Taking acting lessons would probably be the ultimate form of assertiveness training.

Just as with repeated rehearsal, whether done with a "coach" or speaking into a voice recorder, acting lessons can help us to polish our assertive responses and deliver them more comfortably. The more often we respond to conflicts and difficulties with assertiveness, the more comfortable we are likely to become about generally expressing ourselves assertively.

The Principle of Escalating Assertion

In order to keep interpersonal tensions at a minimum, the method of escalating assertiveness is recommended. In this method, we initially offer the "minimal" assertive response that might possibly accomplish our goal and then gradually elaborate our responses, making them increasingly forceful each time we receive a negative response. The goal is to make each successive assertion firmer and more forceful than the previous, while continuing to avoid insult or threat. Escalating assertions can progress from a subtle reminder to a simple statement of preference or a polite request to a firm demand to a statement of intended action. For example, if we are served a very well-done steak after ordering "rare," the following escalating assertion would be appropriate:

Waiter: "Is everything all right?"

Us: "I'm afraid not. I ordered my steak rare and this one is well-done."

Waiter: "But I distinctly remember you ordering your steak well-done."

Us: "There must have been a misunderstanding. Please exchange this steak for one that is rare."

Waiter: "I'm afraid there is nothing I can do about it now."

Us: "Yes there is. Please let me speak to the manager."

Sometimes the most forceful type of escalating assertion contains what is called a contract option, a firm statement of our intended action should our wishes continue to be ignored. This type of message is sometimes necessary before the other person takes us seriously and recognizes that we mean business. A contract option is different than a threat in that it is said in a matter-of-fact (rather than menacing) tone of voice and simply provides truthful information about the reasonable consequences that we intend to carry out if the conflict is not equitably resolved. These types of assertions often take the following form: "If you persist in..." or "If you refuse to...," "You'll leave me no alternative but to...."

Escalating assertions can sometimes be effectively used in making positive statements as well. For example, when another person expresses doubt about our expression of positive feeling or affection, it may be useful to add extra force to our statement in order to make sure that it is appreciated as entirely sincere.

<u>Keeping the Air Clear</u>

Contrary to popular belief, when two assertive individuals have a disagreement it typically does not lead to an aggressive conflict. Instead, they tend to communicate on an adult-to-adult level, openly expressing their feelings, both negative as well as positive, at all times displaying mutual respect. The result is typically either:

(1)   A workable compromise, in which each party agrees to sacrifice something so that the needs of both can be respected; or

(2)   A respectable impasse, where no compromise can be reached but in which each person understands the other person's position and respects his or her right to hold it.

After a mutually assertive interaction, we usually experience a feeling of having engaged in a meaningful dialogue with an individual worthy of our trust and respect who also considers us to be worthy of such. In some cases, it can be useful to actually include in our assertive statement an expression of our respect for the other person and our concern that the relationship not be damaged by the current conflict (e.g., "You know that I think of you like a family member and I certainly wouldn't want anything to change that...").

Our words can give us the power to change our life experience. Responsible assertiveness usually works out best for everyone involved. It provides us with the best chance of achieving our desired goals. It can diminish our sense of helplessness and improve our sense of self-worth. Sharing our feelings and concerns communicates the message that we value our relationship with that other person enough to make our feelings known, to want to keep the air clear. Sometimes saying "no" to requests from others is not a reason to feel guilty, but is instead necessary to avoid the larger conflicts that almost invariably arise when we feel unfairly treated. Expressing our wishes and feelings has the power to relieve us of a great deal of stress, prevent relationships from becoming contaminated by resentment, and allows us to better pursue peace of mind.

<u>Some Cautions About Assertiveness</u>

1.   Although typically the best approach to expressing wishes and feelings, being assertive is in no way a guarantee that we will obtain what we want. Frequently, our only reward is the knowledge that we honored our feelings by making the request, while at the same time attempting to show respect for the other person involved. Whenever we make an assertive request, there is a possibility that it may prove necessary to gracefully accept a refusal. Although we have a perfect right to speak up for our wishes and feelings, others also have the perfect right to decline, and they deserve to have their wishes respected as well.

2.   Not every truthful statement represents a responsible assertion. Statements that are likely to be perceived as insulting or that simply call attention to another person's weaknesses or sensitivity (e.g., referring in some way to a person's limited formal education or calling attention to some past decision that proved unwise, etc.) are aggressive, not assertive. When the truth is used as a "blunt weapon," it is aggressive rather than assertive. Aggressive statements express hostility by presenting information that is insulting or embarrassing to the other person under the pretext of good faith assertion.

3.   Statements that begin "I think..." or "I feel..." or "I believe..." or even "I wish..." are not always assertive. If they proceed to express criticism or insult (e.g., "I think you're an idiot" or "I wish you looked more like your sister"), they are

both unreasonable and aggressive and should not be confused with assertiveness.

4. Attempts to be assertive are only appropriate when dealing with a reasonable person. As soon as the person with whom we are interacting displays unreasonableness (e.g., becomes aggressive, lewd or threatening), the only reasonable course of action that remains available to us is to end the interaction and remove ourselves from that person's presence as quickly as possible. There are limits beyond which attempting to be assertive is inappropriate.

5. Disagreeing with another person's opinion is a special case of assertiveness and calls for careful treading. There is a very good reason that politics and religion are usually considered subjects to be avoided in general conversation. People with strongly held opinions or beliefs ("true believers") are rarely persuaded by even the most well reasoned arguments and tend to find it difficult to accept that others might reasonably hold different opinions or beliefs. When confronted with arguments against their fixed point of view, they simply become more adept at defending it. Tactfulness often dictates that we let a sensitive matter drop and change the subject.

6. There is a big difference between anger and aggression. Anger is a normal emotion that everyone experiences from time to time. Aggression, while often inspired by anger, usually involves abusive behavior towards another person. Anger, on the other hand, does not quite necessarily lead to

aggression. There are always plenty of more constructive, assertive ways to express our anger. These usually require, however, that before responding we pause long enough to engage our rational thought processes. Responding assertively to anger can also require that we address a recurrent annoyance before our anger grows to a point that it might distort our response into an aggressive one. Responding to our anger without thinking, or failing to respond to our anger until we are intensely disturbed, tends to result in overly aggressive responses.

7. When those of us who have tended to be passive and compliant attempt to become more assertive, the significant others in our lives are likely to exert pressure on us to resume our former (and convenient for them) pattern of behavior. A technique called the "broken record" can help us persist in our attempt to be assertive, even in the face of this type of pressure. In the broken record technique, we select one or two thoughts that effectively express our position and then express only those thoughts, no matter what the other person may say. For example, in a conversation with a friend who frequently leaves his dog with others while he travel, and has just announced that he is coming by to drop the dog off, we might choose to respond with the following statement: "I'm glad that I've been able to help you out in the past, but I have other plans and this is not a good time for me to take responsibility for your dog. So I'm afraid you'll have to make some other arrangement." Then, we simply repeat the same response and we refuse to be manipulated into discussing other issues or defending our position.

8. Those of us who like to please others often create problems for ourselves by feeling that we have to respond to requests immediately, which usually means when we're feeling great pressure to acquiesce. Practicing assertive responses that ask for delay, additional time before we are expected to respond, is often a good first step for a person striving to become more assertive. Statements such as "Give me a day to think about that" or "I'd like to sleep on that one" or even "I need a few minutes to think about that" are relatively unthreatening and can be of great value by removing the immediate pressure that often leads us to respond out of habit rather than reason. This type of response is generally underutilized, as all of us tend to perform better after a little reflection.

Examples of Responsible Assertive Statements

1. I know that you're only trying to help, but I really feel more comfortable doing it myself.

2. I may be disabled but my head is working fine. Please respect my decision.

3. I'm completely committed to this relationship. I'm willing to do whatever it takes to make it work and I want to know if you feel the same.

4. I'm not really sure what to say right now. Let me have some time to think, before I make a decision.

5. Before I get so mad that I say things that I don't really mean, I'm going to leave for an hour or two.

6. That's a decision that's too important to make on the spur-of-the-moment. I'd like to sleep on it before I give you my answer.

7. For at least a while, I'm not going to be able to do all of the things I used to do around here. I'd really appreciate any help you can provide.

8. I'm very confused about my medical condition, doctor. I'd greatly appreciate it if you would take a few minutes to explain your opinion about it. What do you feel would be the best treatment plan and what changes can I expect in the future?

9. (To an attorney) I'd greatly appreciate it if you could give me some idea of what I can expect to happen in my legal case over the course of the next few months/years.

10. (To a loved one) You can help me most by just letting me know that you want to be supportive and that you are confident that I will find a way to deal with what I'm going through.

11. (To a loved one who inadvertently upsets us) I know you're trying to help but it really bothered me when you.... In the future, please try to....

12. I hear what you're saying but I'm most comfortable doing it my way. Please respect my decision.

13. (When we have been either inadvertently critical or aggressive) I can see that what I said upset you; I'm really sorry. That was not my intention. I'll try to be more careful and considerate of your feelings in the future.

14. I don't have an answer to that question right now. Give me some time to think about it.

15. I don't like the way this conversation is going. Let's talk about something else.

16. When you say that, it makes me think that you don't care about my feelings, and that hurts, because I want you to care as much about mine as I care about yours.

17. (To a friend or loved one) Please let me know when you notice that I'm trying something new and making an effort to work around my disability.

18. (To a loved one after conflict) I love you. Let's stop fighting, take a break, cool down, try to forgive each other and see if we can begin feeling close again.

19. I would love it if you would give me a hug right now.

20. I know that my disability has been hard for you, too.

I'd really like to feel closer to you again. Even when I get upset, I want you to trust that I will be able to deal with it.

21. I'm sorry if I upset you. I must have said/done/handled that badly. I really was hoping we could clear the air.

22. I have confidence that you'll find a good way to handle that problem and I'll support your decision completely.

23. I'm sorry, but I don't buy from door-to-door salespeople. (Close door)

24. I'm sorry, but I don't contribute to door-to-door solicitors. (Close door)

25. When I tell you that I can't do something because of pain, please just accept that it's true. When you express skepticism, it feels like you're calling me a liar.

26. (To an attorney) You haven't been responding to any of my telephone calls. Would I be more likely to get a response from a fax or email communication?

27. (To an attorney) I've decided I want to go on with my life as soon as possible. Please try to resolve my legal case as quickly as possible.

28. Please ask me before you make a commitment on my behalf.

29. Please lower your voice.

30. Let's discuss this later, in private.

31. I feel like I'm doing more than my share and I'd like to renegotiate our arrangement.

32. I was expecting you to come and was disappointed that you didn't. What happened?

33. This afternoon is not a good time for me. When else might we be able to do it?

34. I'm sorry to have to disappoint you, but I'm in a lot of pain tonight so I won't be able to host our card game.

35. I know that you're trying to help me get better with advice but it ends up making me feel criticized. Please stop.

36. I know that it's difficult for you to talk about problems, but if you'll let me know what's bothering you, we may be able to work out a reasonable solution.

37. I know you're concerned about my well-being, but I'm capable of assuming responsibility for deciding who to spend my time with.

38. I'm sorry that I've disappointed you, but my visit to the doctor this afternoon took longer than expected.

39. It just doesn't seem reasonable, doctor, that you haven't been able to get a response from the insurance company. What other steps can we take?

40. I'm sorry but I won't be able to baby-sit any more. Due to my medical problems, it's much more difficult than I expected.

41. I want you to know that I really appreciate what you've done for me, doctor. I give you a lot of credit for the way you've helped me.

42. It really bothers me when you say critical things in front of others. If you have something to say, please bring it up when we're alone together.

43. Please just leave me alone right now. I need some time to myself.

44. I understand that you have many other clients, but it is very important to me that you do what is necessary to get my medications authorized.

45. Unless you show me that my case is important to you and you can get this issue resolved, I'll have no choice but to begin looking for another attorney.

46. Please speak to me as an equal partner in this relationship.

47. Please ask for my input before making decisions that affect both of us.

48. I'm sorry but I don't buy anything from telephone solicitors. Please take my name and phone number off your list. (Hang up)

49. Doctor, I know you've been doing your best to help me, but it seems as if I'm not getting better. I would really appreciate it if you would refer me to a specialist who might try another approach.

50. I think the information you've been giving me is inaccurate. I'd like to speak to a supervisor, please.

VIII

Making the Most of Relationships

Developing and enriching our personal relationships with mates, children, parents, siblings or friends may represent our greatest opportunity to improve the quality of our life experience, both before and after having become disabled. Research shows that most of us rate our relationships with the people we care about as number one in importance, ahead of jobs, accomplishments, fame or even wealth. Most of us agree that a life without loving relationships is unlikely to feel satisfying or meaningful. Why else would people keep searching and trying, following one painful breakup after another? Human beings are social animals and most of us have a powerful inherent desire to bond with another person.

Although the trauma of becoming disabled can initially cause us to feel like avoiding almost everyone, it cannot long deprive us of our capacity to give or receive loving affection and emotional support. Disability may initially place great stress on a couple, but if we can avoid "dumping" our frustrations on our significant other, it can also provide the time and opportunity to form a stronger bond and pursue greater mutual respect, intimacy and understanding.

In addition to enhancing the quality of our own life experience, loving relationships have strong healing powers. Medical studies have found that involvement in a strong, loving relationship adds an average of five-to-seven years to our life expectancy. Our love for others somehow sends a healing message to our bodies. Being part of a loving couple makes us feel more "connected", "grounded" and "centered" than any other experience, and it is just as possible to attain after becoming disabled as before.

Loving Relationships

The term *love* is used to define many different things. The ultimate goal for most of us is a *loving relationship*, a long-term primary commitment between two adults who honor and respect each other. Though we usually tend to think of a loving relationship as one involving sexually exclusive partners who live together, other types of loving relationships are certainly possible. Most of us depend upon several non-sexual loving relationships with friends and/or family members, a *social support network,* for fulfillment and balance, and to ensure our primary relationship from becoming overly pressured or burdened.

Although sexuality is usually present in a relationship, I feel it is neither a central nor essential element. Many of us confuse being in a loving relationship with being in love or falling in love; a state of infatuation and hormonal excitement that happens to us as the result of our psychosexual biology and that rarely lasts more than six months.

Entering into a loving relationship, on the other hand, is a conscious decision. It is something that we make happen and it represents a long-term commitment. Being in a loving relationship allows us to function to our full potential; being "in love" impairs our ability to function. Being in a loving relationship allows us to think beyond just ourselves and our partners; being "in love" causes us to become preoccupied with ourselves and our partners. Being in a loving relationship makes us become generous; being "in love" makes us become jealous.

Many relationships begin as psychologically immature biological love, or falling in love. Physical attraction sets off hormonal "fireworks" that can trigger an intoxication rivaling that of any drug. If our partner proves to be compatible in terms of attitudes and values, the infatuation can last for months, as we gradually "discover" each other. If it happens that we meet each other's needs, with respect to giving and receiving affection, taking and relinquishing control, liking to be with others, companionship, entertainment, financial advantage, enhancement of social image, sexual pleasure and even the opportunity to have children, the relationship will persist even longer. Yet the most powerful rewards of a relationship, however, don't come from what another person can do for us or from being the object of another person's love. Instead, the greatest gift of a relationship is the opportunity to step beyond ourselves and explore the joy of caring about another person. Being in a primary, mature, loving relationship allows us to become part of something greater than we can ever be alone. Forming a union of the heart eases the pain and sorrow that life inevitably brings.

We form a primary, loving relationship when we and our partner make a conscious commitment to live with one another, support each other, treat each other as equals and respect each other's feelings as we would our own, despite each other's many human faults and weaknesses. The remaining elements and boundaries of the relationship can take many different forms, defined by our preferences and those of our partner, and the compromises that we are able to reach.

__The Ingredients of a Successful Relationship__

In order to survive and prosper, a major relationship requires the presence of five elements:

(1) A commitment by ourselves and our partners to treat the relationship as a precious possession, to abide as much as possible by our mutually agreed-upon relationship rules and limits, and to participate in good faith in attempts to resolve the conflicts and problems that will inevitably arise.

(2) Mutual respect that is communicated by caring about and giving equal consideration to our partner's preferences, wishes and feelings; especially when we're making decisions affecting both of us, but also when making decisions that may primarily affect just us.

(3) Establishing assertive adult-to-adult communication: respectfully, sincerely and consistently making our feelings and wishes known to our partner while avoiding criticism,

blame, threat, "talking down to" or any other form of aggression or disrespect.

(4) Tolerance, acceptance and forgiveness: a willingness to let go of and overlook those idiosyncrasies of our partner that can't be changed or are of little importance, as well as to forgive his or her normal human faults, weaknesses and sincerely regretted mistakes.

(5) Respect for interpersonal boundaries, which is the distinction between each other's private space, personal business and individual responsibilities.

Our most meaningful relationships aren't always with a mate. Relationships with children, parents, siblings or friends can also produce the sense of connectedness, affection, understanding and respect that can enrich our lives and improve our ability to cope with whatever might happen. Even relationships with pets are known to frequently be of major psychological benefit for individuals who have experienced trauma or loss.

Occasionally, after becoming disabled, we will discover that a mature, loving relationship will not be possible with our current partner. When this occurs, we can invest our energies in expanding our relationships with other loved ones, and we may decide to leave the current relationship and seek a more compatible partner. In some cases, this occurs most readily with another person who has become disabled, as there would be a shared understanding upon which a loving relationship might be built.

Although becoming disabled may initially cause many of us to feel so distressed that we don't want to see anyone, it can also provide the opportunity to renew and revitalize relationships that may have faded while we were busy working, or even to find new connections with others who better understand our disabling injury or illness.

Relationship Maintenance

In order to stay healthy and grow, loving relationships require that both partners contribute time and energy to maintain the alliance. Respect for our partner and our relationships means being available to talk and share experiences. This means having the will and ability to participate in our partner's preferred activities in exchange for his or her participation in ours. It also means being willing to call attention to conflicts and problems and to spend time and energy negotiating until a mutually acceptable solution or compromise is found. Potential solutions exist for almost every relationship problem and can be discovered by any couple willing to invest the time and energy searching for the solution as partners, all the while tenderly considering each other's feelings as well as their own.

In a loving relationship, "proving" to our partner that we are right about something often proves, instead, that we are wrong about what's really most important to the relationship. Highly competitive individuals can have successful relationships, but only if they put the goals of the "team" ahead of their own, and root for each other like a good teammate does. In order to "win," both parties must feel successful. There's no such thing as "winning" a relationship conflict if our partner is dismayed by the outcome.

The best resolution to a possible relationship conflict is a compromise that makes both feel that their sentiments in the relationship have been appropriately respected. When no compromise can be found it may sometimes be best to settle differences by random chance, such as the flipping of a coin. The critical element is the feeling that each partner was respected equally in making the decision and that the quality of the relationship has been the highest priority.

Loving Communication

When we form a loving bond with another, we agree to trust each other enough to considerately express our wishes, dissatisfactions and hurt feelings. When there is some kind of conflict in a loving relationship, both partners "put their cards on the table," negotiate, problem-solve and hammer out compromises, all while reinforcing their mutual commitment to treat the relationship as of greatest importance. Relationships tend to work best when we represent our own concerns first, but so strongly value the relationship that we want our partner to feel equally considered. As long as we are both willing to negotiate and compromise in a reasonable manner, some workable resolution is likely to be found, even if it may simply be to decide to respectfully agree to disagree. In any event, we have communicated the message that we value our relationship and the respect of our mate/partner.

Assertiveness in loving relationships means more than just making sure that our statements to our partners are sincere and non-aggressive. What this also means is monitoring ourselves and our partners for signs of conflict or anger and having the courage to bring those into the open, or to call attention to potential problems so that they can be dealt with effectively and we can avoid contaminating the relationship with hidden hostility. We can communicate the message: "Because my relationship with you is important, I want to be honest with you and make sure that this problem gets dealt with."

One of the keys to resolving relationship conflicts is substituting assertive communication not only for aggression, but also for passive-aggressive silence. In order to avoid the risk of provoking conflict, some of us will simply try to overlook inconsiderate treatment by our partners. The effects of passively tolerating unreasonable treatment are almost invariably damaging to a relationship. First, we are perceived negatively for sending the message that abusing our feelings is permissible. At some level, our partner's self-image is damaged by his or her own display of inconsideration and even by our implication that he or she would not respond reasonably to our objection. Furthermore, any unexpressed anger will almost invariably surface later in some form that is likely to harm the relationship. Though addressing our dissatisfactions can surely be difficult, if done assertively and emphatically, it can play a critical role in preserving and improving our relationships.

When dealing with loved ones, its particularly important to avoid certain statements that might be construed as being aggressive. The notion of "constructive criticism" is misleading. In truth, virtually nobody actually wants to be criticized and criticism rarely brings people closer. We are less likely to offend or arouse defensiveness if we can avoid criticizing or complaining and instead simply ask directly for what is wanted (e.g., "Before you leave the house, please let me know where you're going and when I can expect you back."). Even when a criticism might be entirely justified, it is unlikely to have any positive effect on the person being criticized and may do some slight damage to our relationship with that person.

Sometimes we can help our loved ones by letting them know what to do and say when they see that we are in distress. What most of us want when we are in acute pain or distress is for others to appreciate that we're struggling to cope. We want them to be understanding, to support us emotionally and to express confidence in our ability to take care of our problems and meet the challenges of chronic pain and disability. We might ask that when they see that we are in distress, our loved ones say something like:

> *"I'm sorry that you're hurting so much. I want you to know that I am 100 percent behind you and that I'll always be here for you. I have confidence in your ability to handle this situation and to make the best of it."*

<u>Treating Each Other Like Adults</u>

Our communications with others will be most effective when we attempt to act in a responsible, adult-like manner: by addressing the other person as an equal adult and by expecting the same treatment in return. This type of communication is sincere, respectful, empathic and assertive. Neither threats or blame, insults or cursing, commands, scolding or begging qualify as constructive adult-to-adult communication, as each implies a hierarchical relationship that does not exist.

When we engage in adult-to-adult dialogue with a loved one in the hope of resolving a conflict, neither of us may be completely satisfied with the outcome, but we are more likely to reach some type of reasonable compromise that permits each of us to feel that our wishes and feelings have been considered. When we speak "down" to another, as a parent might to a child, we are likely to elicit child-like responses, either rebellious or dependent. When someone speaks "down" to us, the best response we can make is to try to respond with sincere adult-like assertiveness and hope that this encourages the other person to do likewise.

We can become more effective communicators by recognizing that our actions can sometimes send messages that nullify or outweigh the content of the thoughts we express in speech. Just as giving a great deal of attention to a child who is throwing a tantrum is likely to increase the frequency of tantrum throwing, if we repeatedly tell someone that a behavior is unacceptable and won't be tolerated, without taking another step, the stronger message may be that we are tolerating it. In this way, we may some-times inadvertently encourage unwanted behavior in others.

Trying to Resolve Conflicts

Numerous conflicts arise in even the most loving relationships; conflict simply cannot be avoided in human interaction. The preservation of our loving relationships depends not on avoiding conflicts but instead on finding ways to resolve them, with as little damage to the relationship as possible.

Our relationships are constantly changing and these changes can develop into self-perpetuating spirals. By the time a couple enters counseling, their relationship has often spiraled downward to a point that resembles a battleground, with the two partners on opposite sides of the trench and their communications consisting primarily of verbal assaults.

The first goal in attempting to repair a damaged relationship is to establish a ceasefire; to secure each partner's agreement to halt further assaults. Only when the partners can address each other civilly can problems and conflicts be addressed and a pattern of positive exchange and upward spiral be commenced. An extended period of conflict can cause such extreme defensiveness, however, it may be rather difficult for partners to communicate without becoming aggressive in spite of their agreement. Studies have shown that when communication between two partners contain at least five times as many positive expressions as negative ones, the relationship is judged by the partners to be successful. A principal goal to fix a broken relationship is the replacement of aggression with expressions of consideration, respect and caring.

Before deciding that a relationship is beyond saving, we should first test every possibility of rehabilitating it. Both we and our partners have probably invested a great deal of time, energy and emotional attachment in the relationship. Before abandoning what we originally hoped might prove to be a "goldmine," we should thoroughly explore all possible veins of ore. After all, there's no guarantee that our next relationship will work out better, especially if we may be contributing to the problem without recognizing it.

When one's partner is unwilling to participate in relationship counseling, it may indicate that he or she has already decided to end the relationship, but has yet to muster the courage to make a break. Sometimes, however, the unwillingness may simply be a reflection of embarrassment or guilt. This can be clarified by asking that partner, "How can you let this relationship die without first making every effort to save it?" This question is usually best posed by a neutral third party. Unless a relationship has actually deteriorated to the point of some unforgivable act, if both partners are motivated, it may be saved and improved to the point of being mutually satisfying.

Sometimes relationships can be saved and enriched even after serious transgressions, depending on one partner's capacity to forgive and the other's willingness to take major steps to ensure that serious transgressions do not recur. Although anger can become a wall blocking our affectionate thoughts and feelings, it is not incompatible with love.

It is possible to be firmly committed to continue to love a person with whom we are extremely angry, but that commitment may be temporary, unless progress is made toward resolving the conflicts that underlie the anger.

Trying to Fix a Relationship

When we want to improve a relationship or "turn around" a downward spiral, there are some steps that may help, provided both partners are willing to participate:

(1) *Construct a list of our partner's best qualities.* Each partner begins by creating a list of five to ten of the other's most appealing and positive qualities. These are often the same qualities that attracted us in the beginning of the relationship, but we may have lost sight of them during the downward spiral of the relationship. The partners then take turns sharing the other's positive qualities one at a time, ending when either partner's list is exhausted. If one partner still has more positive qualities listed, those should be withheld, or at least reserved, until the other partner has come up with a matching number.

(2) *Express care and consideration.* Each partner constructs a list of ten ways they might show positive regard for the other. These can take many forms, including sincere compliments, expressions of appreciation, statements of commitment, placing an affectionate note in a sock drawer, preparing a favorite meal, sending flowers, writing a poem,

fixing or mending something that's needed repair for a long while, taking responsibility for tasks usually left to the other partner, an unexpected telephone call and so on. Both partners attempt to implement each of the ten items over the next week.

(3) *Eliminate aggression from communications even if it means having no direct conversation.* Before expressing any thought that might be construed as criticism or blame, first consider whether the idea might be better left unsaid. If it is too important to overlook, make sure that the statement made is as assertive and empathic as possible. Ask for what is wanted, without belittling, criticizing or threatening. If aggression or defensiveness creeps into the conversation, stop speaking to each other altogether. Instead, it is wise to temporarily limit all communications to written or recorded messages, these can then be reviewed and revised to delete any aggressive content before they are exchanged. It might help to have a third party review these messages for any aggressive content we may have missed.

(4) *Stay out of the past.* When two people are in conflict, references to the past almost always involve some sort of defensive "mudslinging" that serves no good purpose and simply inserts an additional wedge. The rules of fair fighting specify that, unless it's to express appreciation or a compliment, anything that happened more than twenty-four hours ago is "off limits."

(5) *Avoid making generalizations or absolute statements.*

Statements that begin "You always...," "You never...," "You're a...," or "You're just like...," are usually untrue and destructive to the dialogue and the relationship. Rarely are we so consistent as to "always" or "never" do anything. It is only by carefully noting rare occurrences of a desired behavior on our partner's part that we may find an opportunity to nurture that behavior into a more frequent event. When addressing complaints about the actions of our partners, we should be as specific as possible to time and place. "Last night you..." is much easier to deal with than "You always..."

(6) *Practice responsive listening.* This is a somewhat difficult but highly effective technique in which, before attempting to express our own thoughts or respond in any way to what our partner has said, we attempt to reiterate in our own words what we believe to have been our partner's message and feelings. First, we do our best to hear what our partner has to say. We can make it clear that we are actively listening by establishing eye contact, moving closer, paying careful attention and clearly expressing interest. We also avoid jumping to conclusions or interrupting until our partner is completely finished. We'll get our chance to respond in time. If we feel that it would be useful, we can make some notes as our partner is speaking about what was said, not our defensive response. When our partner has finished and the floor has been turned over to us, we begin by repeating back our understanding of what our partner has said (e.g., "As I understood it, what you said was..."). If our partner feels that we have not completely or accurately received the message, the message is clarified until we are

able to express it in an acceptable manner. When our partner agrees that we have adequately understood his or her message and feelings, it is then we can proceed to express our points.

This process of mirroring the thoughts and feelings expressed by our partner makes it clear that both partners are heard and encourages each to expand on the message until it is well understood. Although the technique can feel strange, it can help us understand more clearly what our partner is actually saying and feeling. By carefully listening to each other and trying to understand what our partner is saying, our relationships can be dramatically improved.

It would be hard to overestimate the importance of careful listening in enriching loving relationships. There are few things that can increase feelings of affection and attachment more than making others feel that we truly want to understand their feelings, and the only way that we can do that is by carefully listening and observing. A client once advised me that because God gave us two ears and one mouth, He must have wanted us to listen twice as much as we talk; good advice to keep in mind when attempting to resolve relationship conflicts.

When one member of a couple is either unavailable or unwilling to participate in relationship counseling, I do encourage the partner who has consulted me to consider what's known as unilateral disarmament. This means refusing to participate further in the battle, attempting to ignore hostile remarks and acting out of respect, courtesy and as much affection as can be mustered in the circumstance. Often at times, the best way to elicit mature behavior from others is often to act in a responsible adult-like manner ourselves with hope that, in the absence of counter-fire, further hostility will seem increasingly unreasonable and will eventually stop altogether.

Tolerance and Forgiving

Contrary to the trite ending of the 1970s classic movie *Love Story* ("Love means never having to say you're sorry"), love actually means repeatedly attempting to show our loved ones that we regret any pain we may have caused them.

Why do we cause loved ones to experience emotional distress? Life can be difficult because we all have faults and limitations and cannot avoid making many mistakes. A life crisis, such as becoming disabled, can temporarily throw us into turmoil and makes it difficult for us to see beyond our own pain and problems. Our loving relationships, however, can survive almost every storm if we do our best to sincerely express remorse when we have behaved inappropriately, show tolerance and acceptance of our loved one's human faults and failings, and we make attempts to be forgiving when sincere remorse has been expressed.

Our human weaknesses can cause almost all of us to occasionally commit the following blunders:

(1) Saying "no" because we feel pressured or powerless, even when we know at some level that the proposed action would probably be for the best;

(2)   Revealing that we find another person attractive, even though we are fully committed to a loving relationship;

(3)   "Dumping" our negative thoughts and feelings on our partner just because he or she is there and it feels safer than sharing them with someone else;

(4)   Having unreasonable expectations of loved ones, or looking to them to solve problems that only we can resolve;

(5)   Overreacting, which means expressing our irritation or annoyance more strongly than is reasonable because we are distressed about something else;

(6)   Having "blind spots" that may cause us to act without regard to how our actions may affect our loved ones.

Each of us is imperfect and we will, at times, blunder in our interactions with our loved ones. For our loving relationships to survive and succeed, we must be aware of this fact, be willing to attempt to forgive and try to do better. Some of us, however, find it too painful to acknowledge our own weaknesses and may attempt to hide our faults and feelings from others, and sometimes even from ourselves. This can make it not only difficult to forgive ourselves for making what may be understandable mistakes, but also makes us more difficult to love. It is our weaknesses, acknowledged and accepted, that can draw us together more closely. When we enter a mature loving relationship, we can then make the commitment to try to cherish our partner in spite of his or her faults and weaknesses. When in conflict with a loved one, it can sometimes help to remember that every aggressive word or defensive act actually represents a misdirected plea for both respect and acceptance.

Because we are only human we will repeatedly provoke anger in each other. Yet we are also capable of finding some way to adjust, forgive and accept each other. Although apologizing may be difficult when we have been in a "relationship war," both partners almost always have plenty to apologize for. By spontaneously beginning to offer "reparations" (e.g., flowers, compliments, expressions of affection, acquiescence to our partner's wishes, etc.), it may be possible to start a positive exchange in the hope of repairing some of the damage done.

Changing Ourselves and Others

One of the most common blunders in all of human relationships is believing that we can change another person. Psychologists and marriage experts around the world have been inundated with complaints about one spouse's inability to "fix" the other one. The common wisdom is that none of us has the power to change another person. Although people sometimes do change, the direction in which that change takes place is unpredictable and the best course is always to assume that no change will occur.

Although we cannot change another person, we do have the power to improve our own attitudes and actions. And by improving these, we may allow another person to reveal the best in him or herself. Although others will rarely do as we wish, our actions will often have a significant impact on the people we care about. If not, how could it be that individuals in loving relationships live an average of five to seven years longer than single people? Rarely is anyone changed for the better by having another person intrude into his or her personal business and responsibilities. On the other hand, almost all of us benefit when our loved ones treat us in a respectful and loving manner, while at the same time working to make the most of their own lives.

What does it mean to treat another person in a respectful and loving manner? In simple terms, it means that no matter how the other person may behave, we do our best to follow the Golden Rule: Do unto others as you would have others do unto you. Although this may be the most widely known rule in the world, it is not one that is easy to implement. If it were, the world would be a much more pleasant and peaceful place. Part of the problem may be human nature. We are born into a potentially overwhelming world in which it can be a struggle to stand up to the challenges and dangers of life, and to find some basis for feeling worthwhile. Some of us have been treated badly and are understandably defensive and pessimistic. Communicating an expectation of the worst from others can be self-protective in that it prevents disappointment, but it can also become a self-fulfilling prophecy that may bring about the negative expectation.

Because we are inherently social beings, we tend to evaluate ourselves in relation to those around us: friends, neighbors, siblings, etc. Perhaps the oldest method of enhancing self-esteem is for a whole group of people to raise themselves above all others. This is why, in some primitive languages, the word for "human being" applies only to members of the local tribe, while members of all other tribes are referred to by another term that means "less than human." The desire to see ourselves in a more positive light is the fundamental source of all human prejudice. "I may not be rich or beautiful or smart, or good at anything at all but, at least, I am superior to all these _____ people." Fill in the blank with any ethnic, national, racial, religious, gender, sexual orientation, political affiliation or other superficial demographic that actually tells us nothing about any particular individual of that group.

As we often discover after becoming disabled, even people who might otherwise seem reasonable and well-meaning are sometimes prejudiced against those who have simply been unfortunate. When a person seems to withdraw from us or treats us less respectfully after we have become disabled, it is usually because it helps that person to feel safer and more secure: "I'm not like that person who got hurt; he must have done something stupid; something bad like that couldn't happen to me." Although this type of self-defensive thinking may explain why others sometimes communicate the message that they consider us to be somehow "less than" them, people who repeatedly communicate this message are generally best avoided, even if that person is a friend or a family member.

When others reject us, it usually says much more about them than it does about us. They may not be in the market for a relationship. They may be too busy, too troubled, too frightened or simply looking for something we can't provide (e.g., wealth, glamour, excitement, etc.). When the act of being rejected by others seems to be a pattern, however, it may be time to look for ways and means to make ourselves more attractive as relationship partners. For example, in order to avoid being perceived as self-preoccupied, we can attempt to balance talking about ourselves with a show of interest in others. In order to avoid seeming negative and pessimistic, we can attempt to balance our complaints about life with expressions of interest and enthusiasm. So as not to be seen as "hard to please," we can attempt to balance our criticism of others with expressions of compassion and understanding. To prevent ourselves from seeming cold and distant, we can attempt to display warmth and affection. In order to avoid being seen as "controlling," we can make it clear that we don't need to have the final say in every decision. In order to avoid being seen as passive and dependent, we can speak up assertively about decisions that are being made. We will always have much greater control over our own behavior than that of others, and we can work to become better and more attractive relationship partners.

Shaping Up Behavior

Although we will always have greater control over our own behavior, there are a number of ways in which we can attempt to influence the actions of others. The most direct of these is obvious--asking directly for the change that we want. If done assertively, this is entirely appropriate. If done assertively in the context of a loving relationship, our request is likely to have a significant impact. Direct appeals by themselves, however, may not always produce or sustain exactly the effect that we are hoping for.

Another method of encouraging sustained altered behavior is a process commonly referred to by behavioral psychologists as shaping. In addition to assertively asking another person to alter his or her behavior, we can also attempt to identify what rewards ("reinforcements," in psychological terms) the current behavior is producing, and how we might be able to change the contingencies so that the behavior we desire would be likely to produce greater reinforcement. Two basic laws of human behavior are:

(1) A behavior will most likely decrease in frequency if it is not reinforced (rewarded) and will eventually stop altogether ("extinction") if it consistently fails to produce reinforcement.

(2) A behavior is likely to recur if it results in reinforcement.

These are "laws" that we have known and used throughout our lives, possibly without recognizing it. We write thank-you notes, express our appreciation for special consideration, and repay favors with kind deeds, all to reinforce behaviors we appreciate and want to encourage. Sometimes, however, we can inadvertently discourage desired behavior by overlooking or failing to reinforce responses that were in the desired direction, but which were incomplete or somehow inadequate. When a loved one displays a behavior that includes some aspects of what we are hoping for, but the behavior goes unacknowledged and unrewarded (no reinforcement), the entire behavior, including those aspects that we liked, tends to be extinguished. By employing the rules of learning we can attempt to "shape" a loved one's behavior by rewarding successive approximations of the desired behavior.

Behavioral scientists, like B.F. Skinner, discovered many years ago that it is possible to teach a pigeon to pull a lever, even though when left to their own devices, pigeons almost never pull levers. It was discovered that by rewarding a behavior that was at least slightly in the direction of lever-pulling (e.g., turning to face the lever) until that behavior was occurring much more frequently. By then, successively holding back the reinforcement until the bird produced a behavior even more in the direction of lever-pulling (e.g., moving towards the lever, then touching the lever, then touching the top of the lever, etc.), a pigeon can eventually be taught to pull a lever whenever a signal light is turned on.

Although our loved ones are more sophisticated than pigeons, by selectively reinforcing those aspects of their behavior that resemble the behavior we desire and then holding back the reinforcement for closer and closer approximations of the desired behavior, we may be able to subtly influence our partner's behavior without resorting to criticism or nagging or appearing to be demanding. For example, if our partner tends to wear odd clothing, it might be possible to compliment one aspect of his or her apparel and explain why we like it, along with the plan of complimenting every subsequent improvement. If our partner sometimes doesn't seem to be listening when we speak we can systematically reward those occasions on which he or she demonstrates that we were heard (e.g., "I really like it that you paid such close attention to what I was saying. It shows me that you're interested.").

Just Desserts

There is a book for women called *Men Are Just Desserts*. I think the title says it all, for both men and women: Put your life and your well-being, not your relationship partner, at the center of your world. Make your life as an independent person as complete and rewarding as possible before being concerned about finding a relationship.

Our ability to successfully create a loving relationship will depend upon how well we have created a fulfilling life experience for ourselves separate from a mate. To begin with, constructing a rewarding life means developing a social support network of friends and/or family members; people that we see on a regular basis for mutual enjoyment and benefit. These people know us, show respect for us, communicate liking and caring, and support for us in times of crisis.

Creating a fulfilling personal life also means developing a set of interests that keep us involved, busy and finding ways to constructively express ourselves (e.g., cooking, painting, crafts, dance, writing, politics, faith-based activities, etc.). It also means developing good self-care habits, including exercise, diet and a healthy lifestyle. Finally, it means finding a way to support ourselves and live self-sufficiently. These steps both prepare us for a rewarding life, with or without a mate, and make us more attractive as a potential mate. They make us more interesting and they lessen the likelihood that a partner will ever feel trapped or helpless. In other words, loving relationships are most likely to succeed when we don't *need* them, but instead *want* them, like a dessert after the main course.

Respecting Boundaries

Healthy relationships also require a mutual respect for personal boundaries, the line that divides one partner's life, experience, business, problems and responsibilities from the other's. Being in a loving relationship can cause us to feel that we have become part of something beyond ourselves, and to a large extent, our life boundaries will overlap with those of our partner. Crossing that line and excessively intruding into our partner's personal business, however, can be the downfall of a relationship.

Some of us have difficulty recognizing appropriate personal boundaries between ourselves and others. This is usually the result of growing up in a home where personal boundaries were not respected and where we had no good models of maintaining separate "personal space."

A number of serious problems are more likely to arise when we fail to recognize and respect personal boundaries between ourselves and others. We may attempt to speak for others, rescue them from their problems, choreograph their lives or even try to protect them from their own responsibilities. Although tackling another person's problems can be a great distraction from facing our own, sometimes the other person's problems can become overwhelming. And in many cases, our intrusion will be resented, causing us to feel unappreciated for our efforts.

Sometimes our interference may deprive the other person of the opportunity to learn how to manage his or her own problems, leading to even greater self-doubt and dependency. An expectation may develop that we will take responsibility for whatever major problems that person encounters in the future. Sometimes the other person feels pressured into going along with our decision, and then subsequently resents our involvement, especially if the action we recommended does not work out well.

The victim-rescuer-villain triangle is a well-known phenomenon among psychologists. It demonstrates the difficulties that are likely to arise when one person attempts to "rescue" another from a major life problem.

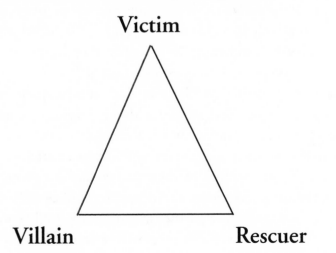

Victim

Villain   **Rescuer**

Although we may initially view the person that we attempt to help as a "victim" and ourselves as a "rescuer," experience has taught us that once a person has been cast in any position in the triangle, at various times he or she is likely to feel or be seen by others in all three positions. The original "victim" may come to resent our intrusion and see us as "villain" instead of "rescuer." Or they may welcome our rescue, expect us to continue to rescue them, and then cast us as a "villain" when we are unable to solve all of their problems. In either event, we may end up feeling like "victim" and we are likely to eventually see the original victim as "villain."

When we're attempting to rescue the "victim" from a third-party "villain," that person will almost immediately attempt to cast us as "villain" and will likely take steps to make us feel like a "victim." If the third-party villain is able to win over the original "victim" to his or her point of view, we are most likely to feel doubly victimized for our efforts to help. This phenomenon is probably the source of the expression "no good deed goes unpunished."

Beyond donating to charities and good causes, it is extremely difficult to help others without creating unintended negative consequences. A good example of this is what often happens when a law enforcement officer attempts to intervene in an incident of domestic violence. These are among the most dangerous and dreaded of police calls. No matter how severely one partner might be physically battering the other, when a law enforcement officer arrives on the scene, the partners often immediately close ranks against the outsider, who quickly becomes viewed by each party as an intrusive "villain." Frequently, the officer becomes an object of violence, ends up feeling like a "victim," and views the battered "victim" as much a "villain" as the batterer.

Even when we have the best of intentions, attempting to intervene in other people's personal business often resolves nothing and may lead to previously unforeseen difficulties.

Some people, usually those who have trouble managing their own lives, feel compelled to straighten out the lives and problems of others. In a loving relationship, this can be extremely annoying and is best confronted in a loving manner, such as, "I know that you're trying to help, and I'm glad that you care, but I need to work this out my way. I'd like you to respect my decision." Taking care of ourselves and disregarding what others may think is not always being "selfish" or "self-centered." Instead, it is quite often being self-attentive in a healthy way.

Boundary confusion can destroy loving relationships as it communicates disrespect of one partner by the other. It can cause one partner to feel "smothered" by the other and can place a great pressure on both partners. Respecting our partner means allowing him or her to be a separate individual, with separate thoughts, beliefs, preferences, problems, business and responsibilities. Telling another person how he or she should think or act is arrogant and disrespectful. It implies superiority and tends to make others feel treated like a child. When we act like a parent to an adult loved one, we may encourage submissive or rebellious, childlike behavior. If we are fortunate, our loved one will respond as a mature adult and politely ask that we stop. Loving relationships benefit from attitudes such as "I see things this way and it's all right if you don't, but don't expect me to change my mind" and "I really want to do this and I'll understand if you don't want to, but I'm going to do it anyway."

Getting our needs met is our own responsibility. Loving relationships work out best when we don't allow our partners to stop us from doing what we feel is best for us and we respect our partner for doing what he feels is best for him or her. Sometimes the best way to reduce stress in a relationship is to "resign" as our partner's manager or to "fire" our partner from the position of being our manager.

So long as it doesn't show disrespect to our partner's feelings, whatever is good for us as individuals is good for our relationship. If we can express our shared pleasure in a loved one's success or good fortune, our love is communicated and our relationship becomes stronger.

<u>Keeping Relationships "Clean"</u>

One of the principal reasons that it is so difficult to prevent primary, loving relationships from becoming dominated by conflict is that our lives become so intricately entwined with those of our partners. We actually have many different relationships with our mates, and conflict in any one of those connections can "contaminate" all of the others. We are typically friends, lovers, housemates, co-owners, travel companions, financial partners and a "couple" for social purposes. We tend to become both teammates (e.g., in bridge or doubles tennis) and competitors (e.g., in backgammon or singles tennis). We will often become a parental unit and sometimes we may even be co-workers, business partners or supervisor/supervisee. And then there are the many other subtle relationships that can develop between mates: cook/food critic, home-user/home cleaner, driver/passenger, etc. It's a major challenge to keep all of these relationships in sufficient repair so that we can consistently be on good terms with each other and easily share support and affection.

Avoiding "confounded relationships" as much as possible is a basic rule of interpersonal psychology. A relationship is considered to be confounded when we have more than one type of interconnection with the other person. A relationship would become confounded, for example, if we became business partners with our father-in-law, became romantically involved with our child's teacher or began playing golf with our therapist. Confounding our original relationship with a second type of connection creates confusion and instability. Entering into a business relationship with a relative or friend can often be seen, in retrospect, to have been the first step in the eventual demise of the relationship, as our feelings about the other person as a business partner can contaminate our feelings about that person as a friend or relative. This phenomenon may explain why siblings often become estranged given their involvement in an inheritance.

Whereas all loving relationships are confounded, it is generally best to keep our relationships as "clean'" as possible. While it is not possible to limit a primary, loving relationship to a single connection, the rule still applies. For example, beginning to work with or for a spouse could cause a major problem in many relationships.

Adjusting to Sexual Changes

Sexual pleasure can be a wonderful part of a loving relationship, and in some instances, it can be so powerful that it is the strongest force holding two people together. I feel it is not the most important (or even an indispensable part) of a mature, loving relationship. When a relationship dies merely because of the loss of a sex life, that relationship was, by definition, not a mature, loving one to begin with.

Illness or injury often has a major impact on sexual activity due to pain and immobility, the psychological impact of disability and/or the effects of medications. While the loss of a sex life can represent a major stress to a loving relationship, by itself it will almost never cause fatal damage.   Mature, loving partners will eventually find alternative ways to satisfy each other's sexual needs or will simply agree to have a sexless loving relationship, with each partner assuming responsibility for satisfying or controlling his or her own sexual impulses in a manner that is acceptable to the other partner. Even when intercourse becomes impossible, loving partners will find ways to provide a great deal of sexual pleasure to each other and can remain active participants in each other's sex lives.

When attempts at sexual intercourse prove too painful or frustrating, a sex therapy technique known as *sensate focus* can be extremely useful. The first step in this hour-long exercise is for the partners to agree that under no circum-stances will sexual intercourse be attempted until after the procedure has been completed. In complete privacy, the partners then take turns (a coin flip works well to decide how to start) at being either "director/receiver" or "stimulator." The director/receiver, either nude or wearing as little clothing as possible, reclines on a comfortable surface and the stimulator begins gently attempting to touch the reclining partner in a pleasurable way. The director/receiver is the one in control, quickly stopping any touch that is unwanted and instructing the partner in what might be preferred. The stimulator can intermittently ask, "Does this feel good?" or "Do you like this?" but it is the director/receiver's responsibility to direct the activity. Sometimes this can be done non-verbally by simply placing our partner's hands elsewhere. The exercise continues for thirty minutes (or until the receiving partner reaches sexual climax, as sometimes occurs) with the goal of obtaining maximal sexual arousal or pleasure. Then the partners exchange places and repeat the exercise in their new reversed roles.

Many of us feel very self-conscious about our bodies. If our embarrassment can somehow be overcome, the sensate focus technique can be an extremely rewarding experience and can represent a first step in overcoming one of the negative impacts of disabling injury or illness.

When to End a Relationship

Although I encourage couples to take every possible step to try to save their relationship (including consulting one or more relationship therapists), not every relationship is salvageable. Being tolerant and accepting can only go so far. Being forgiving of our partners does not mean being willing to tolerate repeated abusive or humiliating treatment. It also does not exactly mean willingness to assume a disproportionate share of family responsibilities so that a partner can engage in a pattern of self-destructive behavior (e.g., alcohol or drug abuse, compulsive gambling, refusing to reasonably attend to serious medical conditions, etc.).

Relationships that have been affected by substance abuse, domestic violence or other recurrent aggressive or self-destructive behavior are particularly difficult to salvage. *No person who is abusing drugs or alcohol is capable of reasonably participating in a relationship or benefiting from any effort to improve a relationship, including psychotherapy and relationship counseling.* For there to be any chance of resurrecting a relationship that is in trouble because of a destructive pattern of behavior (whether substance abuse, domestic violence, compulsive gambling, criminal activity, etc.) both partners must first acknowledge that the behavior is unacceptable. The partners must also agree that the behavior is uncontrollable without an appropriate rehabilitation program (e.g., substance detoxification and rehabilitation, Alcoholics Anonymous, anger management, etc.). Unless the partner, who is repeatedly engaging in some form of aggressive or self-destructive behavior, stops that behavior completely and becomes actively involved in an appropriate rehabilitation program, the most constructive step we can take, for both ourselves and our partner, is to end the relationship. Sometimes, the most loving step we can take in a relationship is allowing the natural consequences of our partner's actions to take place, refusing to condone self-destructive behavior by withdrawing from the relationship. This type of tough love is sometimes the only way we can effectively communicate the message that the offensive behavior is totally unacceptable and that we refuse to enable it further by staying in the relationship.

As is all too apparent from divorce statistics, many attempts at forming a loving relationship fail. No matter how much effort we may put into making a relationship work, without an equal commitment from our partner the relationship is likely to fail. As odd as it may seem, the option of separation or divorce is important to the health of any relationship. People remain in loving relationships because they choose to. Without the possibility of ending an unsuccessful relationship we would be "trapped", a circumstance likely to be damaging to everyone involved.

The option of ending a relationship is very crucial, because we all make mistakes. Sometimes our partners hide disturbing aspects of themselves that become apparent only after we have become a couple. Sometimes we find the relationship so attractive and exciting that we are "blind" to the signs that the other person may not be a reasonable relationship partner. Sometimes we enter relationships with the unrealistic notion that we will be able to change the other person into the partner that we want them to be. All of these circumstances can result in frustration, disappointment and unhappiness. In order to find hope about the future, it is important that we have the possibility of either trying to "do better next time" or living a rewarding life as a single person.

Although the Paul Simon song says that there are "Fifty Ways to Leave Your Lover", ending a relationship is usually very difficult. It may be best for all of us that we have the complete option of ending our relationship, but it is also generally best to keep any thoughts we may have of doing so to ourselves. Mentioning the possibility of separation or divorce to our partner is unlikely to be of any benefit and will probably arouse so much negative emotion that it may be difficult to thereafter work constructively together on any problem. When relationship problems become so severe that we begin thinking of dissolving the union, it will almost always be more productive to keep that thought unexpressed and instead focus all of our energy on trying to resolve the underlying conflicts or problems. This may mean further dialogues between the partners or even seeking the assistance of a relationship therapist. It is premature to speak of ending a relationship, however, until we have exhausted every possible avenue of resolving the conflict and we are firmly convinced that it will not be possible to have a healthy relationship with this partner. Any mention of separation, divorce or otherwise ending the relationship, however, is best deferred until we have reached the point that we are prepared to actually take the step. Once a partner asks to end a relationship it may never again be as secure and loving as it was before.

Once we have made the decision to end a relationship, it is almost always best to avoid sending any mixed signals. As long as a relationship is alive, all energy is best focused on trying to keep it alive and make it work for both partners. Once the decision has been made to end it, however, all energy is best concentrated on making it clear that the relationship is over and we're moving ahead in life as a single person. When it is our partner who has decided to end the relationship, usually the best thing we can do is to try to respect that decision, recognize that for some reason it was not meant to be, and put all energy into moving ahead in life as a single person. When a partner ends the relationship because we became disabled, it's a pretty good sign that we really didn't have the relationship we thought we had to begin with.

Having a partner end a relationship can be an extremely painful experience. Usually the only reasonable response is to try to accept the decision, turn to our social support network (friends, family members, clergy, therapist) for emotional support and try to keep ourselves as active and involved in personal interests as possible. Refusing to accept the decision and continuing to attempt to "win back" our partner shows disrespect, both for that person as well as for ourselves.

Ignoring a partner's request for an end to a relationship is similar to the recurrent expression of jealousy—it achieves nothing worthwhile and can make us seem disrespectful, pathetic or even disturbed. When the partner ending the relationship is ambivalent and repeatedly gives mixed messages (for example, spending time interacting with us after asking for no further contact, delaying in moving out, continuing to discuss how the relationship might have been saved, wanting to "still be friends," etc.) frustration can grow into intense anger.

Every human being has many faults and weaknesses, and any relationship can be fragile. When we suffer a disabling injury or illness, the delicate balance of our relationship is often thrown askew and we may then discover limitations in our loved ones that were not previously apparent. Although disability can initially place our relationships under great stress, our capacity to develop a rich, loving relationship can remain intact despite physical incapacity.

Most of us care about the impact we have on the people we love. We want their respect and confidence. By responding to disability by acting in our own best interests, we can create the impression of resilience. Forgiving ourselves and others for causing the disability creates the impression of tolerance. By trying new activities that might be able to replace those that have been lost, we can create the impression of adaptability. By letting go of what we can't control and finding new ways to make our lives more fulfilling, we can create the impression of wisdom. Refusing to surrender to passivity and despair creates the impression of courage. And in the process of creating these positive impressions, we can explore the limits of our full potential and know that we have changed for the better.

Relationships are a process; they never stop changing. If neglected, they will deteriorate. When nurtured, they will thrive. The mutual effort and consideration required to overcome the challenges created when one partner in a relationship becomes disabled, it can actually "fuse" a relationship, making it stronger than ever before. *This is one of the ways we can win the disability challenge.*

IX

The Pursuit of Feeling Well

Our health, physical and emotional, is the foundation for our experience of life. For those who believe in the human spirit, our bodies are its "temple," the physical structure on which our ability to accomplish anything depends. The better we maintain and nurture ourselves the more capable we'll be of bouncing back from trauma and loss. Becoming disabled makes it more crucial than ever that we focus time and energy on activities that will promote health, manage pain and increase feelings of well-being. Only by making our health the object of our loving care and attention can we test the limits of our body's capacity for recovery and provide ourselves with the best chance of successful mental adjustment to the long-term effects of illness or injury.

This chapter will offer information and recommendations with respect to pain management, exercise and diet, managing panic and insomnia, developing relaxation skills and identifying when professional health consultation might be appropriate. A comprehensive discussion of these topics is beyond the scope of this book, however, and most all health-related decisions should first be cleared with a qualified physician. Reference will also be made to other sources that can provide information in greater breadth and depth.

<u>Managing Pain</u>

Chronic pain can be one of life's toughest challenges, and one that most of us who have become occupationally disabled face everyday. As we continue to search for medical solutions to our pain problems, we hope for further spontaneous healing. It only makes sense to also search for non-medical "tools" that can be used to better cope with and alter our pain experience. Although we may not be able to eliminate the pain, we can become experts at managing its impact on our lives.

Chronic pain can trigger a chain of reactions that leads to a number of potentially serious problems:

1) *Excessive inactivity.* We sometimes respond to persistent pain by avoiding any activity that might precipitate or exacerbate our pain. As a result we may become inactive, out of shape and more prone to both new injury and further aggravation of old injury.

2) *Helplessness and depression.* Until we have developed an arsenal of pain-management tools and a corresponding plan of action, we may experience feelings of helplessness and suffering that can trigger a depressing cycle of thought.

3) *Overuse of medications.* In our efforts to avoid pain, we may sometimes overuse medications, some of which can cloud our thinking, impair our judgment and rob us of the energy and motivation needed to reclaim our lives.

4) *Excessive preoccupation with physical sensations.* Persistent pain can cause us to become so concerned about our physical health that every foreign sensation can seem to indicate the onset of a serious decline in our health.

5) *Social isolation.* Persistent pain can cause us to become so irritable and others can sometimes be so insensitive that we often become withdrawn, isolated and even more discouraged than ever.

Fortunately, all of these problems can be avoided or corrected by developing an arsenal of pain-management weapons, a broad collection of techniques that we can incorporate into a "battle plan" for combating and coping with pain whenever we encounter it. The more techniques and abilities we can apply to the management of our pain, the less we'll be deterred from accomplishing our goals in life, the healthier our lifestyle will be.

We can begin to counteract the difficulties that chronic pain presents by making a contract with ourselves. First of all, we can decide to accept the fact that our pain is primarily our problem. No one else—not doctors, not even our closest loved ones—will understand or care about our pain nearly as much as we do. It is up to each of us to assume responsibility for exploring every possible option that can help us manage our pain. Accepting ownership of our pain and leadership in our efforts to conquer it acknowledges that we are worthwhile and deserving, that there is a reason to do everything we can for our comfort and well-being and that we still have plenty of options to choose from.

Pain experts agree that a well-developed strategy employs as many approaches to pain control as possible. Examples of such programs would be likely to include:

1) *Anti-inflammatory and/or analgesic medications.* Although it usually takes more than a prescription to manage pain well, medications can certainly play an important role in our efforts to live with pain. Because some of us are reluctant to take narcotic pain medications, at times we either take too little to optimally manage our pain level or we delay in taking the medication until our pain level has risen to the point that the medication is much less effective. Others among us will overuse medication in an attempt to avoid experiencing any pain at all, resulting in impairment by side effects. In order to keep either our pain level or medication side effects from reaching a debilitating level, narcotic analgesic medications are best used on a regular schedule, precisely as directed by our treating physician.

2) *Improve fitness.* If we want our bodies to treat us well, it only follows that it would be best to treat them as well as possible. Initiating a gradual program to improve our

physical conditioning, beginning with easy activities (e.g., walking ten minutes on a treadmill) followed by some gentle stepwise increases, can improve our fitness and, correspondingly, our pain tolerance.

3) *Keep a pain diary.* By recording the nature and level of our pain several times each day, we can better learn how to avoid exacerbations and what techniques are most helpful and acquire a greater mastery over our pain.

4) *Develop a set of distracting activities.* Keeping as busy and active as possible is often the best antidote for both pain and sorrow. Occupying our minds with hobbies, work, crafts, artwork, puzzles and special interest type of constructive enterprise can actually reduce pain. Studies of the most severe types of chronic pain have found that challenging mental activity was the most effective treatment. Keeping our hands and eyes busy with distracting activities (e.g., hobbies, work, crafts, artwork, puzzles and/or other special interest involvements, volunteer work, etc.) can "push" our pain into the background of our perception. On the other hand, when unoccupied, our brains become fully dedicated to the perception of pain. The more we can distract ourselves, however, shifting our attention to something else, the less our brain focuses on pain and the less we perceive it.

5) *Develop better relaxation skills.* Methods such as progressive muscle visualization, relaxation, meditation, biofeedback therapy and self-hypnosis can reduce muscle tension and thereby relieve pain. A positive mood and peace of

mind seem to activate the immune system and make us stay healthier and feel better. Anxiety and tension, on the other hand, interrupt the immune system, making us more susceptible to illness, premature aging and aggravate pain.

6) *Non-pharmaceutical pain control methods.* Treatments such as acupuncture, massage, hypnosis and chiropractic manipulation are known to have helped many, at least temporarily, control pain. Hot and cold applications, mechanical braces and electrical stimulators can also be helpful. We can also make our homes and offices as ergonomically correct as possible by using chairs with good lumbar support and positioning our computer keyboard to allow our wrists to be neither bent up nor down. The utilization of a wrist pad so that as we operate the keyboard our wrists are lying on the pad rather than a hard tabletop, can also be extremely beneficial.

7) *Avoid states of deprivation.* For many of us, being "tired and hungry" equates to being "mean and nasty" and to experiencing greater pain. We can make it a point to take frequent breaks, alternating rest with activity in a pattern that prevents our pain level from becoming too severe. At the first sign of increasing pain we can respond by taking "downtime." We can learn our most comfortable positions and assume those as frequently as possible. We can learn how to alternate positions and activities to best manage our pain level. Also, we can pace our activities carefully, and in planning them we can allow plenty of time for rest and intermittent breaks.

8) *Develop our social support network.* We can work at strengthening our social support network. This group consists of friends and relatives that we can count on to be supportive and can be of great help in a crisis. We can also strengthen our social support by developing new relationships with individuals who may have special understanding of our medical condition and disability.

9) *Develop a daily schedule.* We can organize our day around the management of our pain, including each of the various pain-management tools that we plan to utilize on that particular day. And we can also list constructive, meaningful activities that fall within our physical capacities.

10) *Consider the use of other types of medications.* Clinical levels of anxiety, depression and insomnia are known to heighten our perception of pain. Sometimes our pain level can be improved by the use of medications to treat those conditions.

11) *Respect ourselves.* We can work at letting go of our concerns about what others may think, while at the same time attempting to assertively confront disrespectful behavior. For example, we might respond to an insensitive relative: "When you express skepticism about my pain and impairment, it feels like you're calling me a liar. When I tell you that I can't do something because of pain, please just accept that it's true. You can show me that you love me by trusting what I say and displaying concern for how I feel."

12) *Continue pursuing personal goals.* We can refuse to let pain stop us from the pursuit of our personal goals. Viewing our recovery as the accomplishment of our goals after a long, difficult struggle will therefore be more valued than something that was passively bestowed upon us by some external force.

13) *Find a "pain coach."* Having a health professional to consult, at least intermittently, can help us to clarify the information we've heard, better understand changes in our symptoms, keep abreast of new medical innovations, plan our pain-management strategy, make appropriate specialty referrals and make us feel less alone in attempting to manage our pain. This person could be a physician specializing in pain management, another type of medical specialist, a physician's assistant, a Nurse Practitioner, a physical therapist, a chiropractor or a psychologist or psychotherapist who specializes in pain-management.

Pain is a serious health issue in its own right, not just a reflection of some underlying physical problem. Whereas physical pain is often unavoidable, suffering (the emotional reaction to pain) is optional. We suffer when we allow pain to trigger fearful thoughts, feelings of helplessness and anxious worry. If we can respond with a plan of action, we may be able to manage the depressing cycle of thought that pain often produces and avoid the sensation of suffering.

If you are looking for a more detailed approach to managing your pain, I recommend *Managing Pain Before It Manages You* by Dr. M.A. Caudill. Dr. Caudill offers a fully comprehensive program designed to help any individual cope with chronic pain.

Healthy Relaxation

If we can improve our ability to relax, we can both diminish pain and improve our overall health. Studies have shown that just two minutes of relaxation repeated several times each day relieves stress and improves our health. By sitting back or reclining in a comfortable position, closing our eyes, breathing slowly and regularly, consciously letting the tension flow out of our muscles and imagining a pleasant scene, we can induce a health-promoting state of relaxation. By repeating this two-minute exercise throughout the course of each day, we will feel better, have less pain and live longer.

Certain activities have been found to induce relaxation, diminish muscle tension and change body chemistry for the better. Almost all of these involve forcing ourselves to be in the "here and now," as opposed to thinking about the past or future.

Meditation and other "mindfulness" techniques are known to induce relaxation and a sense of well-being. These techniques generally involve four basic elements:

(1) *A quiet environment.* Meditation can take place at home, in the garden, at a place of worship or in the outdoors, as long as the setting is peaceful and free of unpleasant noise.

(2) *A comfortable position.* It's best if the position can be comfortably sustained for twenty minutes. Sitting down is usually preferred because many of us fall asleep if we are reclining.

(3) *An object to dwell on.* This can be a simple syllable (e.g., God, love, ohm, etc.) or a longer mantra that is repeated over and over, a symbol that is gazed upon or perhaps even a particular sensation or feeling that is contemplated.

(4) *A passive attitude.* This is an emptying of thoughts and concerns. Let the conscious mind relax; there is no right and wrong about which thoughts and images come and go, drifting through our awareness.

More can be learned about mindfulness and meditation from *Full Catastrophe Living* by Dr. John Kabat-Zinn.

Breathing techniques have documented benefits for both health and relaxation. One of the easiest of these is slow pattern breathing, in which we exhale slowly for as long as we can, pause until we begin to feel uncomfortable, inhale slowly until our lungs are full and then pause again before slowly exhaling.

Imagery or *visualization* refers to the process of creating a mental picture, a scene in our "mind's eye" that can serve as a powerful tool for improving both relaxation and performance. Sports psychologists have found that athletes perform best both when they are relaxed as well as after repeatedly picturing themselves succeeding.

Disciplines such as yoga, Tai Chi and other choreographed movement routines such as the Japanese Tea Ceremony require us to focus concentration intently upon our physical movement. They can draw us out of the part of our brain that worries, thereby easing mental tension and improving our relaxation. Biofeedback and self-hypnosis training also have documented relaxation benefits.

In *progressive muscle relaxation,* we systematically tense and relax each of our muscle groups, while reclining in a comfortable position. Practicing this technique can make us more aware of our body's tension and become more skilled at releasing it.

We can learn to feel better, have less pain and improve our health by creating as vivid a peaceful scene as possible and putting ourselves there: "seeing" the beauty, "hearing" the sounds, "feeling" the atmosphere, even "smelling" the sweetness. Even though we may actually be in the dentist's chair having a tooth drilled, in our minds we may also be able to put ourselves hundreds of miles away, under a tree on a hilltop, seeing clouds dotting the blue sky above the forest, feeling a cool breeze stirring the leaves and passing over our face and arms, hearing the sounds of the wind and the birds, smelling the cedar and eucalyptus and staying relaxed. Furthermore, by picturing ourselves coping with difficult life events or circumstances, sort of "day dreaming" of struggling or battling but getting through and attaining success, we are able to, in many cases, actually enhance our real life success.

Taking Care of Ourselves

The American Heart Association tells us that there are six steps that we can take to live healthier and longer:

1) *Stop smoking.*
2) *Keep cholesterol level low.*
3) *Keep blood pressure under control.*
4) *Keep blood sugar under control.*
5) *Get/keep weight under control.*
6) *Manage alcohol consumption.*

Most of us recognize that smoking damages our health, but nicotine is a very addictive substance and it takes strong motivation to stop. Nevertheless, if we are sufficiently motivated there are a number of smoking-cessation programs that will probably be effective. When we're ready to try, we can consult our personal physician or contact Nicotine Anonymous (415-750-0328) or Smokenders (800-828-4357).

Controlling cholesterol, blood pressure and blood sugar requires us to work closely with our personal physicians, although we can also make an impact through better exercise, diet and weight control --all of which are discussed below.

Although alcohol can numb pain, it is a very poor medication. Pain studies have found that alcohol actually increases pain for some patients. Alcohol also contains a lot of calories without any nutritional value. More than two evening drinks can disrupt our sleep pattern by reducing deep sleep and dreaming stages, leaving us not rested in the morning. Excessive alcohol consumption can damage the liver, pancreas and brain. In the long run, attempting to use alcohol to treat chronic pain typically leads to far more severe physical and social problems. If we have ever felt that we should cut down on our drinking, been annoyed by people criticizing our drinking, felt bad or guilty about drinking, or had a drink first thing in the morning to steady our nerves or get rid of a hangover, it would be wise to seek medical help.

When we find that we are unable to control a self-defeating habit or addiction, such as excessive alcohol consumption, there are treatment programs and self-help groups that can be of great assistance. No one who is in the habit of drinking excessively is capable of making positive strides in improving our life or solving life's problems. Anyone who is unable to stop drinking (using another addictive substance or engaging in some other self-destructive, compulsive behavior) is likely to benefit from consulting a physician or seeking the assistance of a twelve-step program such as Alcoholics Anonymous.

Exercise, Diet and Weight Control

Controlling our weight is a struggle for most Americans. We have two main tools at our disposal in the battle against the waistline and the scale: exercise and diet. Although other factors may influence our calorie consumption and expenditure, in order to lose weight we ultimately have to burn more calories than we consume. Regular exercise not only improves physical and emotional health, but is the only healthy method at our disposal for increasing the number of calories that we burn.

The first step to developing an exercise program is to find those types of exercises that are most enjoyable and/or least aversive. We are unlikely to become regularly involved in an exercise activity that we dread. For many of us, the best type of exercise is walking. As human beings we were meant to walk, and walking is known to produce a number of health benefits. Furthermore, it's pretty much always available, relatively painless and can even be quite enjoyable, especially in scenic surroundings or while listening to music or a compelling recorded book.

For those of us who are lucky enough to be graceful, dancing can also be an enjoyable aerobic exercise that improves heart and lung function, while burning calories, which can be really quite enjoyable. Certain sports, like tennis and racquetball, can also provide us with exercise as we enjoy ourselves. Some people prefer using indoor exercise equipment, such as stationary bicycles, treadmills, hyperbolic gliders, rowing machines or stair-steppers. Others prefer outdoor activities such as swimming, skating, hiking or bicycling. In certain seasons and locations, activities such as cross country skiing, ice skating, canoeing or kayaking can provide enjoyable aerobic types of exercise.

Although it may not be the most enjoyable type of exercise, it is possible to get aerobic exercise without any equipment or even leaving our home. By simply stepping up one step, then back down, then stepping up with the other foot, then back down, and repeating this over and over for about twenty minutes or more, we can produce an exercise benefit equivalent to using a stair-stepper machine. Walking up and down flights of stairs can also have aerobic benefit, although somewhat tedious to most of us.

What's important is to find exercises that we enjoy enough that we will be willing to engage in them regularly. Having several different possibilities can allow us to exercise during the day or the night and in good weather or bad, while also protecting us from the strain of repetitive motion.

Another critical factor in starting an exercise program is to make sure that we don't hurt ourselves or trigger discouragement. The first time that we engage in a new exercise activity it can seem relatively easy, and there is a risk that we will do too much and cause ourselves a great deal of soreness. It's far better to start slowly and only gradually increase our time and effort so that we only experience a minimum of pain or soreness.

The level of effort at which we begin exercising will depend upon our physical condition at the time. Should there be any question about our physical capacity for exercise, the issue should be clarified with our own physician.

Our first goal is to identify some exercise activities that we find to be enjoyable enough that we are willing to devote at least thirty minutes a day, at least three days each week.

It is often a good idea to dedicate only thirty minutes to exercise every other day, but initially put forth real effort only every fifth minute. For example, if the exercise is walking, we would try to walk at a relatively high speed for one minute, followed by four minutes of more leisurely walking, followed by one minute of faster walking and so on. In thirty minutes, we will have walked rapidly for six minutes and leisurely for twenty-four. If this activity seems too easy we can increase our "leisurely" walking pace, but still walk more rapidly every fifth minute. When we feel ready to increase our effort, we can change the ratio of our two paces so that we are now walking rapidly for two minutes followed by three minutes of leisurely walking. By gradually increasing the period of our rapid walking, we may eventually become able to walk rapidly for the entire thirty minutes. If we then want to increase the level of our exercise even further, we can walk faster or for a longer period of time. We could also attempt to jog intermittently as we walk, provided that our medical limitations permit jogging. By following the same pattern of gradual expansion of the relative time we are engaged in the more demanding activity, we might eventually attain the ability to jog for the entire thirty minutes.

When it comes to dieting, the goal is to develop a healthier lifestyle rather than "go on a diet." Temporary diets tend to produce temporary results. Weight management programs that work involve long-lasting changes in routine activities. These steps can be helpful:

1) *Start a food diary.* Recording everything we eat has been shown to both improve our food choices and reduce amounts consumed.

2) *Limit fat consumption.* Fat contains nearly twice as many calories as carbohydrates.

3) *Eat slowly.* It takes the stomach about twenty minutes to signal the brain that it is full. Eat slowly and delay when taking second helpings.

4) *Find weight loss and exercise partners.* Making a commitment to another person will increase our motivation and our desire to succeed.

5) *Keep a number of low calorie foods on hand.* Having low calorie foods such as carrots, celery, low calorie crackers, sugar free gelatins and puddings, diet sodas, etc., can facilitate in making good choices.

6) *Don't skip breakfast.* As surprising as it may seem, studies show that when we don't eat breakfast we tend to more than make up for it with what we eat later in the day. It's best that we consume the most calories earlier in the day and eat as little as possible in the evenings.

7) *Don't get too hungry.* By eating small amounts frequently, we may be able to avoid the feelings of deprivation that drive many of us to eat excessively.

8) *Remember that "fresh is best."* Processed foods usually have either fat or sugar added.

9) *Remember, "Everything in moderation."* It's best not to forbid ourselves any type of food completely, but to instead make it a special treat in small amounts.

10) *Don't let the scale win.* We can't control what our weight does; we can only control our own actions. If we develop a program of exercise and diet and manage to follow this with a reasonable consistency, that should be looked upon as a "success," no matter what the scale may say.

11) *Remember that no one ever follows a diet or exercise plan perfectly.* We all slip at times. That isn't failure! As long as we get back into the program each time we make an error, we can't be defeated.

12) *Remember that, when it comes to eating, almost everything is "normal."* No matter how extreme our lapse—eating a gallon of ice cream at 3:00 a.m. or ordering five fast-food cheeseburgers, etc.—it's been done before by many others and it cannot represent "failure" if we don't give up.

13) *Search for ways to burn more calories.* Remember that for an average person an additional thirty minutes of walking each day will make a twenty pound difference in weight at the end of the year.

Weight Watchers offers an excellent food plan for those of us who would like help and support in our weight loss efforts. If we find that we're unable to control our eating sufficiently to reasonably follow a food plan, help is available through Overeaters Anonymous. For anyone wishing to read more about weight control, I would recommend the *Fit or Fat* series by Covert Bailey, a retired fitness guru whose CDs, DVDs and books have helped countless folks to lose weight.

Flexing Our Brains

Most of us who have sustained disabling injury or illness at some time begin to feel that our cognitive capacities are slipping away. We often find ourselves becoming forgetful, having difficulty concentrating and becoming easily confused. We lose the car keys. We run into a friend but can't recall his name. We suddenly discover that we have driven three miles past our turn. We try to explain something but can't find the word that we need. Suddenly in the middle of a conversation we're forced to stop because we can't remember what we were talking about. The good news is that these problems are rarely a sign of organic brain damage. Typically they are the combined effect of increased distraction by emotional factors, the disruption and disorganization of our usual routines and the effect of medications. When we find ourselves encountering these lapses more frequently than ever before, however, it's understandable that we become alarmed.

Fortunately, there are ways to compensate for these problems and even to improve our cognitive functioning. Sometimes just knowing that our symptoms are understandable (and learning that we probably don't have Alzheimer's Disease) can be a relief. More importantly, we can become increasingly adept at coping with and compensating for these disruptions of concentration and short-term memory.

We can learn to depend less on our memory and begin writing down everything that's important for us to remember. We can begin carefully keeping and consulting both a day calendar and a daily "to do" list. We can improve the organization of our living space so that everything has its proper place, thereby preventing clutter from adding to our confusion. Finally, we can attempt to accept our growing imperfections as simply a normal cost of living and aging, and see if we can find a way to laugh about the silly mistakes that we will inevitably make. After all, almost all of us will eventually be challenged by the problem of adjusting to age-related change in our capacities.

The good news is that for the most part we retain our normal cognitive ability as we get older. The bad news is that we tend to lose our speed and our ability to spontaneously retrieve information from our memory bank. On tests of intelligence, older people generally do just as well as younger people unless the task is timed or requires memory recall without benefit of any cues or prompting. Older people, however, do just as well as younger people on tests of recognition memory. In other words, if asked for a specific name, an older person may not be able to produce the answer spontaneously, but if presented with a list of ten possible answers, the older person is just as likely to select the correct answer as a younger person. We don't lose information; we simply lose part of our capacity to retrieve it.

Medical research has demonstrated that by challenging our brains we can actually change brain structure and raise our intelligence to some extent. A long-term study of one order of nuns (who donated their brains to science) found that those who regularly engaged in challenging activities (such as taking classes, playing chess or bridge, engaging in handicraft or art work) developed denser cerebral nerve connections than those who were more passive and less challenged. In other words, we may be able to strengthen our brainpower by performing mental exercises just as we can increase our physical strength through physical exercise.

Mental exercise can help us improve our memory, concentration and problem-solving abilities. Any activity that forces us to think logically, focus concentration, develop a strategy, sort, calculate or create is likely to contribute to greater brainpower. Some of the more common types of mental exercises that are likely to be helpful are activities such as solving a word search puzzle, completing a crossword puzzle, putting together a jigsaw puzzle, playing a thinking game such as Scrabble or chess, taking a class at the local community college or adult school, attempting to learn a new language or how to play a musical instrument or memorizing a poem or some other literary passage.

There are also a number of other steps that we can take to try to make sure that our brains are working as well as possible. A number of medications (including those for pain) can sometimes interfere with our cognitive capacities. When this occurs we can consult with our treating physician regarding the possibility of altering the dosage, replacing the medication with one that would be less likely to cause cognitive impairment, or change the schedule of administration. Exercise increases blood flow and oxygen to the brain, and has been shown by research to improve verbal fluency. Although some sleep medications may make our memories worse, getting enough sleep is also important for maximal brain functioning.

Combating Sleep Disturbance

In order to find enough energy to cope with the many stresses that are usually created by becoming occupationally disabled, we will probably need a reasonable amount of sleep. For most of us, a healthy sleep pattern involves a minimum of seven to eight hours of sleep each night, with at least two episodes of deep sleep. This pattern is called "restorative sleep" and we depend upon it to feel rested and refreshed upon awakening in the morning.

Unfortunately, many of the symptoms commonly associated with becoming disabled (e.g., pain, grief, anxiety, depression and worry) are likely to disrupt our usual sleep pattern and we can become sleep deprived and less efficient as a result. Although temporary sleep problems are unlikely to cause any permanent damage to our body or brain, they often result in considerable temporary impairment of our ability to function. We can find ourselves feeling sluggish, less alert, forgetful, moody, easily exhausted and unable to sustain concentration. Perhaps most importantly, sleep disturbance can impair our effectiveness at coping with the challenges of disability.

Most physicians will readily prescribe sleep aid medication. Before turning to a drug-induced remedy, it is usually best for each of us to make a first attempt at non-medical sleep management. There are a number of steps that we can take to improve our sleep pattern while at the same time possibly diminishing our feelings of helplessness by doing any of the following:

(1) *Establish a regular sleep schedule.* We sleep best when we go to bed and get up at the same designated time every day. Set aside a seven to eight hour period (e.g., 11:00 p.m. to 7:00 a.m.) as "sleep hours" and do not allow ourselves to sleep outside those hours, no matter how tired we may become. Although it may be difficult to avoid napping, especially for the first two or three days, developing this type of "sleep-wake rhythm" may be critical to the resetting of our body's "sleep clock" so that we can sleep better at night.

(2) *Let it be "okay" not to sleep.* As much as we may want to get to sleep, it's almost never essential that we do. A sleep-less night may be unpleasant and inconvenient, but it's not a catastrophe. Research has shown that, when necessary, we can function very well even when sleep-deprived and that we quickly recover our usual capacities once we have caught up.

(3) *Plan to be awake during the night.* Have activities scheduled in case sleep does not come quickly. We can limit our frustration about not being able to sleep by avoiding prolonged periods of "trying" to fall asleep. We tend to become increasingly anxious as we lay awake, with the result that sleep becomes less and less likely. If still awake after twenty minutes of attempting to sleep, it's usually best to rise, go to a different room and engage in some planned activity (e.g., reading, watching a recorded show, writing a letter, working on a hobby, etc.) for thirty to forty-five minutes before returning to bed and attempting to sleep again. If still awake twenty minutes later, repeat the process.

(4) *Make the bedroom as comfortable and quiet as possible.* Take steps to eliminate light and noise that can interfere with getting to sleep. Even when an external noise cannot be eliminated, we can improve insulation or even purchase a sound-generator to "screen out" distracting environmental sounds.

(5) *Use your bed only for sleep (and sex).* As much as possible, avoid using your bed for any activities that are not directly related to going to sleep. Reading, eating, watching television or doing paperwork in bed creates an association with mental activity that can interfere with full relaxation.

(6) *Exercise regularly.* Twenty minutes or more of aerobic exercise (e.g., rapid walking) each day often improves our sleep pattern. Some people find, however, that it's best to exercise before evening so that the body is not too "revved up" to sleep at bedtime.

(7) *Avoid caffeine or other stimulants (e.g. coffee, tea, soda, chocolate, etc.) within six hours of bedtime.*

(8) *Avoid drinking alcohol near bedtime.* Although alcohol may help "put" us to sleep, more than two drinks can block normal brainwave variation, preventing us from deriving the full benefit of sleep and possibly causing us to feel unrested in the morning, even if we have been asleep all night.

(9) *Avoid eating a heavy meal or drinking large quantities of fluid within four hours of bedtime.* Gastrointestinal discomfort and having to urinate can both disrupt sleep pattern.

(10)   *Create a relaxing bedtime routine.*   For example, develop a routine of taking a warm bath, reading something inspirational, listening to calming music, writing in a journal or performing some type of relaxation-induction exercise (e.g., breathing exercises, imagery techniques, progressive relaxation, meditation, etc.)

(11)   *Put troubles "on hold" until the following day.*   Before going to bed we can take an inventory of the problems we're facing and construct a list of actions that we might be able to take the following day to help resolve them.   "Capturing" problems on paper can sometimes help us to let them flow out of our minds, thus making it easier to sleep.   If we continue to be awake and troubled about problems, we can write out a more extensive plan of how they might be resolved in the future.   When we can think of nothing further that can be done to try to resolve problems that are disturbing us, we may be able to simply "let them go" or "turn them over" to a higher power.

(12)   *Get proper medical care.*   Sleep disturbance is sometimes the result of a biological condition (such as clinical depression) that changes our body's internal chemistry. When this is the case, medications can be helpful and would best be discussed with our personal physician.

When serious sleep problems continue to rob us of our energy and focus even after we have made sincere attempts to follow non-medical approaches of the type described above, it is probably time to consult a physician about a trial of sleep medication.

<u>When Panic Strikes</u>

Anxiety is a complex set of biological and emotional changes that occur spontaneously and involuntarily in reaction to environmental stress, either sudden or prolonged. Although it is a survival mechanism that prepares us for "fight or flight," when it becomes chronic it is damaging to both our bodies and our minds. For most of us, becoming disabled produces considerable anxiety and the relaxation methods discussed above are likely to be helpful. More frequently than is widely known, however, we experience anxiety in the form of attacks that seem to come out of the blue.

Panic attacks are sudden and unexplained episodes of intense anxiety. They often include feelings of impending doom, rapid heartbeat, shortness of breath, sweating, dry mouth, cold hands, chest pain, tingling, and/or nausea and are among the leading causes of emergency room visits. Anxiety can produce terrifying symptoms that can be indistinguishable from a life-threatening medical crisis. It's not surprising that we often respond by calling 911 or rushing to a hospital. After a couple of expensive episodes of being told that our symptoms are "just" the result of anxiety, most of us try to manage them without medical attention.

The biggest danger of panic attacks is that we may start avoiding places or circumstances that we fear might set one off, even though there is nothing particularly frightening or dangerous about those situations. If this pattern persists long enough, we can gradually restrict our movements until we are completely housebound by fear, also known as agoraphobia. One way we can prevent this from happening is by refusing to run when a panic attack strikes. Instead, we will be better off in the long run if we can stay where we are (or find a comfortable spot nearby to rest) and remind ourselves that this is *just another panic attack*. It won't kill us and it will probably pass before long, especially if we're able to practice the techniques that we've found to help us relax (e.g., breathing exercises, imagery, progressive muscle relaxation, reciting the Twenty-third Psalm, etc.). The goal is to make the panic attack as unimportant as possible and to create a memory of having overcome the difficulty at the site of the attack. If we can do this, we also display that we have *courage*, which is possible only when we're frightened, but we nevertheless follow the course of action that we believe to be for the best.

Another method of attempting to cope with anxiety that has had some success is to engage in a distracting mental activity, such as attempting to count all of the windows in our childhood home. For those of us who possess sufficient physical capacity, another technique that has proven successful is to rapidly begin engaging in strenuous physical activity (e.g., sprinting, doing jumping jacks, etc.) at the first signs of a panic attack. During an attack, our body is behaving as though we were already engaged in strenuous activity: breathing hard, heart racing, sweating, etc. Giving ourselves a reason for these symptoms can help us regain a sense of control and can also reassure us that we are not experiencing a medical catastrophe. As is also true with pain, it is best to attend to and treat anxiety as quickly as possible, before it builds to a severe level where treatment is likely to be less effective.

In especially persistent and severe cases of panic disorder, psychotropic medications can sometimes be quite beneficial. Psychotherapy can also sometimes help us identify and resolve the suppressed anger that is usually considered the principal cause of panic attacks.

When to Seek Professional Help

Most of us who become disabled also find ourselves battling depression and anxiety, two natural results of major life disruption and increased uncertainty about the future. When we find ourselves feeling overwhelmed and unable to mount a good effort to cope due to lack of energy, concentration or emotional control, it is probably time to consult either a physician, therapist, psychologist, psychiatrist, clinical social worker, psychiatric nurse-practitioner or some other type of licensed psychotherapist. Each therapist is different and finding one that we work well with is often more important than therapeutic orientation. Therapists can help us "shrink" overwhelming and confusing problems into more manageable portions, prioritize and plan problem-solving strategies. They can teach us techniques for managing our emotional state and point us in directions that are likely to bring greater satisfaction and peace of mind. They can sometimes help us become aware of the ways that we   inadvertently trip ourselves up and make our problems worse. In addition, they can provide emotional support and reassurance as we get through a difficult time.

Couples therapy can be particularly helpful when our

relationship has become strained. Group therapy can be a more affordable means of obtaining a therapist, while also having the opportunity to make a special limited connection with others who are likely to have similar problems. Becoming connected with other disabled individuals can be especially helpful, as they are likely to share some of the same feelings and experiences and may be in a better position to support and encourage us in our efforts to build a more rewarding life. People protest that they simply "don't need to hear about anyone else's problems," but a good therapist will never let a group deteriorate into a "complaint fest."

Some problems of mood are related to changes in central nervous system chemistry. Psychiatric medications can sometimes be helpful in restoring healthier nervous system functioning, even when the clinical symptoms have been brought on by stressful circumstances. Medications can sometimes help us to regain normal energy, motivation and emotional control, and can make it more possible for us to manage our life problems and avoid creating further stressful circumstances. When we find ourselves unable to consistently sustain an effort to cope with the difficulties facing us or we continue to experience disturbed moods even after it seems we have been working hard to cope, consultation with our personal physician or a Board Certified Psychiatrist would probably be worthwhile. Although they can take several weeks to produce benefits (and side effects can sometimes require trials of several different medications before the most appropriate one is found), antidepressant medications can play a big role in improving mental health.

If an antidepressant is helpful, it should be taken on a daily basis, for as long as the prescribing physician recommends and at least until the life circumstances that triggered the depression in the first place have improved. There are many depressed patients who have reported that an antidepressant medication led to improved mood, increased energy, greater emotional control and/or improved concentration. Anti-depressants are actually the second most commonly prescribed medication in the country! Experts also believe that approximately twice as many individuals would benefit from anti-depressants as are currently taking them.

By taking the best possible care of ourselves, learning how to effectively respond to pain and anxiety, and taking advantage of professional help when it is indicated, we can prepare ourselves to make the best possible adjustment to disabling injury or illness, and to the other obstacles that life may throw into our path.

X

Epilogue

Life is difficult under the best of circumstances and can seem overwhelming when we become disabled. Although losing our capacity to work is a major emotional stress, it is a crisis rather than a catastrophe. Whatever losses our disability may cause, we continue to have unlimited opportunity to grow.

Once we are able to fend off the feelings of hopelessness and loss that disability often produces, we can see that there are numerous possibilities for improving our life experience through our own actions. By finding inspiration and motivation in the courage that others have shown, and in our love for those who are important to us, we can begin taking active steps in pursuit of positive experience.

By keeping our focus on living one day at a time and letting go of what is beyond our control, we can reduce our feelings of helplessness and improve the moment-to-moment quality of our lives. By giving ourselves credit for the steps we manage to take and forgiving ourselves for what

.

we have failed to accomplish, we can begin each day fresh and focus our energy on taking further constructive action.

By persistently repeating this pattern of hope, inspiration, letting go, forgiveness and perseverance in the face of adversity we can gradually shift our life experience in a more rewarding and self-fulfilling direction.

By responsibly speaking up for ourselves and actively managing our self-defeating thoughts, we can assume greater control over our lives, diminish feelings of helplessness, develop a greater self-assurance and further enrich the quality of our experience. By attending to our personal health, we can optimize our chances for recovery and successful adjustment. Furthermore, by making the most of our relationships with friends and loved ones, we can build a network of social support.

Although it may not be easily recognized, each person who becomes disabled has the opportunity to use that event as a turning point from which life can be made more purposeful and fulfilling. We may have been an unfortunate victim of disabling injury or illness, but we never lose the power to influence the events of our lives, shape our future and promote our recovery. The challenges that are presented by occupational disability can be surmounted.

Appendix A

A Guide to Disability Benefits and Rights

Almost all of us are eligible for some type of financial, medical and/or other living assistance benefits when we become too disabled to work. The benefits that might be available can vary, however, depending upon the nature and severity of our disabling medical condition, what caused it, our usual occupation, our employer, insurance coverage, duration of impairment and even work history. Disability systems can also vary from state to state, county to county and even city to city. Because of these variations, and the fact that disability benefits are continually changing, this discussion will focus on how to obtain additional information, how to file applications and how to locate community resources that can provide assistance. Although an attempt has been made to ensure that the information presented is as accurate and current as possible, both changes and mistakes are inevitable. This guide is best employed as a starting point from which an investigation into potential sources of disability assistance can proceed.

First discussed are the types of aid that tend to be most immediately available when a person becomes disabled, like time-limited disability programs and workers' compensation systems. Next described are long-term disability programs such as Social Security and disability retirement systems. This is followed by a summary of federal laws protecting the rights of the disabled.

Appendices B and C provide information on locating needed assistance and support.

The Most Immediate Sources of Financial Assistance

When personal and/or sick leave employment benefits are unavailable or have been exhausted, the "first line" of disability benefits, those that we are likely to qualify for and receive within the first few weeks after becoming disabled, are workers' compensation systems, state disability systems, public employee disability systems, disability insurance policies and employer-sponsored salary continuation programs.

If the onset of your disability is recent and you are not receiving accrued leave pay or any disability benefit, check with your employer's Human Resources or Personnel Department about the possibility that you may be covered by an employer-sponsored disability benefit or income replacement program. Some large employers offer a salary continuation benefit or even a sick leave contribution program that allows other employees to share unused sick days with a coworker who has become disabled. Most public agencies have internal temporary disability programs that provide benefits for at least a limited period of time.

State Workers' Compensation Systems

Each state and U.S. territory has a system of workers' compensation that requires employers to provide medical and disability benefits to employees who sustain work-related injury. Employers have agreed to take on this legal responsibility in order to limit their liability from negligence lawsuits in the civil courts.

Although workers' compensation laws differ from state to state, they are typically "no-fault." Benefits are provided no matter who may have caused the injury, so long as it meets the legal criteria for "compensability." The benefits provided typically include medical treatment, a temporary partial income replacement and compensation for permanent loss of earning capacity. The temporary living benefit is intended to support an injured worker whose injury prevents the performance of the worker's usual job or any other work assignment that the employer is willing to provide. The amount of the temporary total disability benefit is specified by state regulations, but is often considerably less than the injured worker's usual after-taxes wages. The permanent disability benefit is designed to compensate the injured worker for wages lost in the future due to diminished earning capacity. In many cases, however, the amount of the permanent disability award may not come close to matching the future earnings actually lost due to the injury.

Individuals who have become disabled as the result of a work injury, (including those resulting from repetitive trauma, stress and/or toxic exposure in the workplace), are likely to be entitled to medical and disability benefits from the employer, usually through workers' compensation insurance coverage. Although employers are generally required by state law to provide an injury claim form to any employee who requests one, the filing of claims is sometimes discouraged and employers may occasionally even adopt a hostile attitude toward employees who file claims. Nevertheless, on-the-job injuries are almost always best reported and there are laws to protect injury claimants from reprisals. If making a good faith injury claim causes an employer to become hostile or discriminatory, it may be time to consider seeking employment elsewhere. In any event, doctors are often required by law to report industrial injuries, so an injured worker may not be able to prevent an injury claim from being filed.

Before filing a claim, it may be a good idea to first discuss the causes of your disabling medical condition with your doctor. Medical evidence supporting the industrial nature of the injury is usually required for a claim to be approved. Concerns about high Workers' Compensation costs and a great deal of media exposure about people who have feigned injuries have led some states to impose severe penalties for filing fraudulent claims and have also created considerable (and usually undeserved) prejudice against injured workers.

If an employer fails to supply an industrial injury claim form after one has been requested or fails to provide medical attention or disability benefits after a claim has been submitted, information and assistance can be obtained directly from the state workers' compensation board or from an attorney who specializes in workers' compensation law. It is not always necessary for an injured worker to retain an attorney. When a claim is accepted, the employer/insurance carrier may be very helpful to an unrepresented injured worker. Without an attorney, however, it may be difficult to be certain that the employer/insurance carrier is fully providing all entitled benefits.

Once an injured worker has filed a claim form, the employer/insurance carrier typically has a limited amount of time to accept or reject liability. If liability is accepted, the employer (usually through an industrial insurance carrier), becomes responsible for providing disability benefits and payment of reasonable medical expenses. If a claim is denied or a dispute arises over some aspect of the benefits being provided, the injured worker may find it prudent to seek court intervention or legal representation.

When a treating or evaluating physician concludes that an occupational injury has reached a point of probable *maximum medical benefit* from treatment, the medical condition is declared to be permanent and stationary. At that point, temporary disability benefits are usually discontinued, although they may be replaced with an allowance to live on while completing vocational rehabilitation or a much lower permanent disability benefit. The employer/insurance carrier will most likely assume that once the injury has been stabilized by treatment, the injured worker has regained the capacity to perform some kind of income-producing employment.

When a work injury makes it impossible for an employee to return to his or her usual occupation, some states require the employer/insurance carrier to provide either an alternate position with duties that fall within the medical restrictions, or vocational rehabilitation (retraining for a new occupation that is compatible with the residual disability.)

There are now a few organizations and internet websites that may be of interest to injured workers. The best of these particular sites is most likely WorkCompCentral (http://www.workcompcentral.com). Although there are charges for some of their services, they provide free access to posted information and an opportunity to post questions that will most likely be answered by some knowledgeable individuals.

The Federal Workers' Compensation Program

The workers' compensation system that covers federal employees (FECA) is different than the state programs. It is administered by the Department of Labor's Office of Workers' Compensation Programs (OWCP) and benefits are paid from the budget of the injured employee's federal agency. No insurance companies are involved.

To initiate an occupational injury claim, a federal employee must submit a "Notice of Occupational Injury" (Federal Form CA-1) or "Notice of Occupational Disease" (Federal Form CA-2). The injured employee's physician must submit a corresponding "Attending Physician's Report" (Federal Form CA-20). It is important that the correct forms are used, as submitting the wrong application form can result in the denial of a legitimate claim.

If the correct forms are then properly completed and

submitted (usually to an injury management officer at the injured employee's federal agency) and the agency does not dispute the claim, OWCP will accept the claim and begin paying medical and disability benefits within a few weeks. Federal workers who become disabled due to occupational injury receive two-thirds of their usual gross wages or 75 percent if they have dependents.

If the agency denies the employee's claim, reconsideration can be requested by a Department of Labor Hearing Officer. It can take months, however, before a hearing takes place and the injured employee often must present persuasive evidence above and beyond his or her own testimony. These cases involve one branch of the government reviewing decisions that have been made by another branch.

The structure of the federal system places considerable control in the hands of the federal employee's agency, setting the stage for problems if the injured employee is not on good terms with his or her supervisors. In cases where the supervisor is believed to be the cause of a stress-related psychiatric injury, the employee's best hope of having the claim accepted may be to pursue a corresponding EEOC (Equal Employment Opportunities Commission) complaint of discrimination or harassment. The evidence collected in connection with the EEOC investigation can then be presented to the Department of Labor Hearing Officer who is considering the appeal of the claim denial.

Although injured federal employees have the right to retain legal representation, there is no provision in the federal Workers' Compensation law (FECA) that guarantees payment for legal expenses. As a result, attorneys who work in this area of law often require an advance retainer from the injured worker.

There is also a National Association of Federal Injured Workers *(http://nafiw.tripod.com)* that may be able to provide more information and/or assistance.

Disability Insurance

Some employers offer disability insurance as a benefit of employment, often as a paycheck deduction plan. Self-employed persons often purchase disability insurance. Some disability policies provide benefits when the covered person becomes medically unable to perform his or her usual occupation. Others pay benefits only when inability to reasonably perform any job is established. This can be a major distinction, as it is much more difficult to qualify for benefits under the second type of plan.

Once we have become disabled, having purchased long-term disability insurance can seem like a stroke of genius. When we have chosen not to pay for disability insurance and then we become disabled, we can try to forgive ourselves for not being able to foretell the future and remind ourselves that the decision must have seemed like a good one at the time.

If our disability is the result of an off-the-job accident, we may be eligible for medical and/or disability benefits through some type of liability insurance coverage—automobile, homeowners or business. If we are unable to determine if we are entitled to benefits of this type or if we believe that we are not being properly compensated, it may be best to consult an attorney who specializes in personal injury law. Sometimes having insurance coverage just means having someone to sue when something horrible happens.

State Disability Programs

California, New Jersey, New York, Hawaii, Rhode Island and the Commonwealth of Puerto Rico have state-sponsored disability insurance programs that can provide partial wage replacement for a limited period of time. Typically sponsored by payroll deductions and employer contributions, state disability systems are usually limited to disabled individuals who are not receiving any other type of income. As indicated above, some large employers and public agencies offer their own disability benefit programs and are exempt from the state disability programs.

To apply for state disability benefits or to obtain further information, inquire at the appropriate local program:

California	(800) 480-3287
New Jersey	(609) 292-2680
New York	(518) 474-6680
Hawaii	(808) 586-9188
Rhode Island	(401) 222-3600
Puerto Rico	(809) 754-2119

For those of us who are covered, it may be a good idea to file a claim for state disability benefits even if we're already receiving some other source of temporary disability benefit.

State disability may provide a supplemental partial disability benefit. And, if a state disability claim has already been filed, it is often possible to quickly begin collecting state disability benefits if other benefits are suddenly discontinued. Furthermore, state disability claims often must be filed within twelve or eighteen months of the last day of active work. Filing a claim within that period of time may be necessary in order to preserve our eligibility for state disability benefits beyond the usual deadline for filing a claim.

Some disabled workers who don't qualify for disability benefits may be eligible for unemployment benefits, temporary compensation for individuals who are "between jobs," but who are looking for work. In order to qualify for unemployment, however, it may be necessary to establish that you had good reason to leave your previous job and that you are capable of working. A letter from your doctor stating that you left your job for medical reasons and that you have been released to pursue work that falls within your medical limitations may be sufficient.

Long-Term Disability Programs

In some cases the same programs that provide immediate or short-term disability benefits will also provide long-term benefits if the occupational disability persists. Private disability insurance policies often provide coverage until age sixty-five, although some policies limit the term of coverage for certain types of disability. State workers' compensation programs generally provide compensation for lost future income, although the available benefit may be quite limited.

The Department of Labor maintains that the federal workers' compensation system is "not a retirement program" and urges federal employees who have become chronically disabled to opt for a disability retirement. Federal statute requires, however, that full disability benefits be provided as long as the injured employee remains too disabled to reasonably take part in vocational rehabilitation or perform any job that his or her federal agency offers.

Social Security Disability Benefits

In addition to its better known old age retirement and Medicare programs, the Social Security Administration (SSA) also manages the country's two largest disability benefit programs, Social Security Disability Insurance (SSDI) and Supplemental Security Income (SSI). SSDI is a monthly allowance that is paid from the Social Security Trust Fund and is intended to protect working men and women from becoming impoverished if they become medically disabled before qualifying for the old age retirement benefit. SSI, on the other hand, is typically a more limited benefit that is paid from general tax revenues to disabled individuals who have not made the minimum contribution to the Social Security Trust Fund necessary to qualify for SSDI.

To qualify for SSDI we must have made a sufficient contribution into the Social Security trust fund within the previous ten years and we must establish that we meet Social Security guidelines for both occupational disability and financial need. If our claim is approved, the monthly benefit received will be determined by the amount of our total contribution up to a specified maximum (at the time of writing approximately $2000 per month). Each minor dependent of an SSDI recipient is also eligible for a separate monthly benefit.

Claimants who can establish both disability and financial need, but who have not contributed the necessary minimal amount into the Social Security Trust Fund to qualify for SSDI, will be awarded SSI. In effect, SSI is a federal support system for individuals who are disabled due to either mental or physical impairment, but do not meet the requirements to qualify for SSDI. The exact amount of the SSI benefit depends upon the claimant's state of residence, as certain states supplement the federal SSI payment slightly, but at present is not above $900 per month in any state. Furthermore, to qualify for SSI, total household income and personal assets must both be very limited.

The Social Security Administration offers a confidential on-line screening tool that can help us determine what disability benefit we qualify for. The Benefit Eligibility Screening Test (BEST) can be found at *http://best.ssa.gov*, as can a great deal more information about Social Security benefits and rules.

There are several ways to apply for the Social Security disability benefit programs. A "Social Security Benefit Application" can be filed on-line at **www.ssa.gov**. An application can also be requested from the Social Security Administration by telephone, mail or in person at any local Social Security office. The address of the local SSA office can be found in the federal government listings at the front of the white pages of the telephone directory. If some more assistance is needed to complete the application, an appointment can be made to consult, in person or by phone, with a Social Security representative who can help complete the application. Many communities also have advocacy groups that provide assistance to individuals applying for SSDI or SSI. Some of these are listed in Appendix B.

When we initially apply for Social Security disability benefits, we can expect to be asked for a great deal of personal information, including our Social Security number, proof of age, proof of age for each dependent minor, names and addresses of doctors and hospitals, dates of our medical treatment, the names of all our medications, medical records, information about employment and our most recent W-2 Form or federal tax return, etc. *Do not wait to file your claim until you have collected all of the requested information.* Additional information can be provided after the claim has been filed.

Because the date of application can determine the date on which benefits begin to accrue, it is best to apply as soon as it becomes apparent that you will be occupationally disabled for more than five months, *even if you hope to recover and return to work before becoming eligible.* SSDI was designed to be a "safety net" to protect a disabled worker from becoming destitute or homeless. Even if we are receiving another disability benefit, such as Workers' Compensation or state disability, applying for SSDI at the earliest possible time will help put the safety net in place. Too often temporary disability benefits are discontinued before the disabled individual is able to return to work and before the SSDI claim has been approved, leaving the

claimant without any income at all. SSDI may also partially supplement a disability benefit that is being received from
another source.

Medical evidence confirming disability is critical to
obtaining approval of an SSDI or SSI application.
Claimants are advised to submit the names and addresses of
all doctors who have treated them for any purpose, orthopedic, internal, psychiatric or other medical condition. Social
Security may arrange a medical examination, but these tend
to be superficial and are seldom given much consideration if
more compelling medical information is made available.

Although the Social Security Administration states that
it requires only 90-to-100 days to initially process a disability claim, many legitimate claims are initially denied, often
allegedly due to lack of sufficient medical documentation of
total disability. Claimants who persist in appealing an
initially denied claim are often eventually able to obtain a
reversal, but doing so can take a year or more. When an
SSDI claim is finally accepted, benefits are paid
retroactively to a date five months after the disability is
determined to have started.

When a Social Security claim is denied, a letter must be
sent within the time limit specified in the denial letter,
requesting that the claim be reconsidered. Each and every
time a denial letter is received, a letter requesting an appeal
of the decision should be promptly submitted. These
response letters will keep both the claim and the initial
application date "alive." Should we fail to respond to a
denial within the specified deadline, the claim dies. A new
claim can be filed later, but it will then have a new, and

much later, application date, and some of the retroactive benefits to which we are entitled may be lost.

Social Security maintains a list of disabling medical conditions that are considered so severely disabling that they automatically qualify an individual for SSDI or SSI benefits. If our disabling medical condition is not on the list, we will be required to establish that our medical condition is of equal severity to one of the conditions on the list. Simply becoming unable to perform the type of work that we have done in the past does not automatically qualify us for SSDI. If the Social Security disability evaluator determines, after taking into consideration our medical condition, age, education, past work experience and transferable skills--that we are able to adjust to some other type of work, our claim will be denied. On the other hand, if the Social Security disability evaluator is persuaded both that our medical condition precludes our usual type of employment and that we are adjusting to some other type of work, our claim will be approved. In that case, a retroactive payment of benefits will be made and monthly benefits provided. Monthly benefits will continue so long as we continue to meet Social Security criteria with respect to both disability and financial need. If benefits are being received when full retirement age is reached, the SSDI benefit automatically converts to an old age retirement benefit, but the amount remains the same.

Social Security disability claimants are permitted to designate a representative to assist them in their dealings with the SSA. This person can, but does not have to be, an attorney. Although some non-attorney representatives charge a flat fee, most attorneys take a percentage of the retroactive disability award as payment for their services. Although this may be advantageous to the claimant in that no immediate out-of-pocket cash outlay is required, the attorney's percentage can become a considerable amount if approval of the claim is long-delayed. Although an attorney can assist a claimant in collecting medical documentation of disability and by making sure that no appeal deadlines are missed, many claimants wait to retain legal representation until the SSA has scheduled an administrative law hearing, the stage at which many denied claims are approved.

In my experience, psychiatric disability can represent a critical element in obtaining approval of an application for Social Security benefits, even in cases involving considerable primary physical disability. In order to qualify for benefits an individual must be found disabled with respect to all accessible occupations and there are some types of work that can be performed even by individuals with serious physical disabilities. A secondary depression or anxiety disorder, however, can prevent a person from being able to sustain sufficient energy, concentration or emotional control to function reasonably even in positions that might otherwise be possible. The additional psychiatric disability can be the difference between denial and acceptance.

I have also found that many disabled workers are so invested in regaining their ability to return to work that they are reluctant to apply for Social Security benefits. They often feel humiliated by their inability to work and equate accepting SSDI with an admission of irreversible disability. These feelings are irrational and are best ignored. If we qualify for SSDI, it is because we worked hard enough to pay a sufficient amount into Social Security and we have developed major medical impairment. *Qualifying for SSDI does not mean that we cannot later return to work.* Many SSDI awards are for a closed period of time, beginning at the end of the five month "waiting period" after the initial date of disability and ending with a return to work. SSDI benefits can easily be discontinued if we return to work and can also usually be quickly restarted if our attempt to resume employment proves unfeasible.

In order to encourage SSDI and SSI recipients to re-enter the work force, Social Security offers "work incentives" that preserve disability benefits during trial periods of work. Earnings during the first nine months of a work trial do not affect SSDI benefits at all and the SSDI recipient is allowed to continue receiving the full SSDI benefit for each subsequent month that earnings fall below what Social Security considers to be "the substantial gainful activity level." While this rate is frequently adjusted upward to compensate for inflation, at the time of writing an individual receiving SSDI could earn up to $860 per month without any reduction in his or her SSDI benefit. Individuals receiving SSI benefits, on the other hand, are restricted to much lower earnings—at the time of writing only eighty-five dollars per month—before their monthly SSI benefit is affected.

If the Social Security Administration determines that we have become capable of "substantial work," the SSDI benefit is paid for three additional months and then discontinued. The SSDI benefit can be reinstated any time within the subsequent thirty-six months, if earnings fall below the monthly limit.

Alternatives to Social Security Disability

Many government employers and employees do not pay into the Social Security program, and instead make contributions into public employee disability and retirement systems. Most government employees who have met length of employment qualifications are covered by a disability retirement program.

Employees of the federal government (including the U.S. Postal Service) can become eligible for one of two types of disability retirement programs offered by the U.S. Office of Personnel Management (OPM). To qualify for either program a federal employee must establish only that he or she has become medically incapable of performing the duties of his or her usual job and has not turned down an offer of reasonable accommodation. Minimum civilian federal service is required for eligibility, eighteen months for one program and five years for the other. The eligibility requirements for the federal disability retirement programs are less stringent than those for SSDI, but benefits may be lower. To apply for disability retirement, a federal employee must submit a retirement application (Standard Form 2801 or 3107) to the Office of Personnel Management at 1900 E. Street NW, Washington, D.C. 20415-1000. A copy of the application and more information can be obtained at the OPM website: *www.opm.gov/retire.*

Most state and local public employees are covered by a public employee retirement system that includes benefits for permanent disability. Two types of disability retirement benefits are typically available: one for individuals who have become disabled as the result of medical conditions that are unrelated to their employment and another that pays a higher rate of benefit to individuals who have become disabled due to medical conditions that are determined to have resulted from job-related injury or illness. It is typically much more difficult to qualify for the latter type of disability retirement benefit and the services of an attorney who specializes in public retirement (ERISA) law may be helpful.

The Veterans Administration (aka Department of Veterans Affairs) provides disability and medical benefits to former members of the United States military services who have become disabled as a result of military service, whether combat-related or not. The amount of the monthly disability benefit depends upon the severity of the impairment, which may be periodically re-evaluated and adjusted. In special circumstances it is possible to obtain service-related disability benefits even many years after military service has been completed. Acceptance of a delayed claim, however, will require compelling evidence of a service-related injury or illness that has progressed to the point that it has resulted in some degree of chronic disability.

Having battled anxiety and alcohol problems for more than thirty years after being traumatized during combat in Vietnam, one of my clients was recently awarded a 40 percent service-connected disability and VA medical benefits. After requiring psychiatric hospitalization as a danger to himself and others, another of my clients had his service-connected psychiatric disability increased from 10 to 60 percent. Individuals who believe that they have a medical disability or require medical care as the result of an injury or exposure sustained while on active duty in the military should consult the Enrollment Coordinator at the nearest VA healthcare facility.

Other Benefits and Resources

Victims of Crime

Many states and/or counties have established programs to aid crime victims and their family members if they require medical treatment or become temporarily disabled as a result of the crime. Benefits are typically restricted to expenses that are not payable by any other source. Crime victims who are disabled or require medical or psychiatric care as the result of the crime should ask at the district attorney's office if they might be entitled to assistance from a victims of crime program.

Medicaid and Social Services

When all other avenues of financial assistance have been exhausted, the last resort may be the local, state or county social services department. Families with children may be eligible for basic living assistance and healthcare sponsored by federal Medicaid funds. Adults without children may be eligible for a minimal general relief benefit, Medicaid healthcare benefits and food stamps. Recipients may be expected to refund whatever benefits they receive if they subsequently return to work or receive a monetary award from another source (e.g., SSDI, workers' compensation, etc.).

Medicare and Medicaid

After twenty-four months of accepted disability covered by SSDI benefits, recipients become eligible to receive *Medicare* hospital and medical insurance. There is no charge for the hospital coverage, but if we want the outpatient medical insurance and the prescription drug plan, we must enroll and allow Social Security to withhold a premium for each from our SSDI benefit. Individuals whose claims for SSI are approved become immediately eligible for *Medicaid*, federally-funded, state supplemented health insurance coverage that often restricts an individual to medical treatment at public and/or non-profit health facilities.

Individuals who become eligible for Medicare coverage sometimes find that they can obtain more comprehensive and/or cheaper medical coverage by assigning their Medicare benefits to a private health insurance company or HMO. It may also be possible to secure more favorable insurance coverage by agreeing to pay an additional premium. To explore these options, we can contact the health insurance company or our local HMO in which we might be interested.

Affordable Housing

The United States Department of Housing and Urban Development (HUD) offers programs to assist disabled individuals and their families obtain affordable housing. Many cities participate in a HUD program that helps disabled individuals purchase a first home. More information can be obtained from the HUD website at *www.hud.gov*, at your local city hall or even from some local real estate agents who specialize in these types of transactions. The United Way sponsors a "dollar matching" program to help those in need (families whose income is less than double the federal poverty guideline) purchase a home. For more information, we can regularly check the United Way website at *www.unitedway.org*.

Although not widely known, some states offer modest financial assistance to disabled renters or homeowners in the form of a partial property tax refund. For example, in California the Franchise Tax Board will "refund" several hundred dollars per year to assist a disabled resident with rent or mortgage payments. To obtain more information we can call our state or county tax offices.

Some states also sponsor assistance services by caregivers or housekeepers for individuals whose disabilities prevent them from being able to perform these functions for themselves. For more information, we can check with our state or county social services department. We can also check to see if our utility and/or telephone service providers offer discounts to disabled customers.

Vocational Rehabilitation

Most states sponsor vocational rehabilitation programs designed to either help disabled individuals find work that is compatible with their medical limitations or to acquire skills that would make alternative employment possible. SSDI and SSI recipients are typically automatically eligible for these services (see Appendix B). For more information, contact your state rehabilitation office.

Disability Rights and Advocates

The *Americans with Disabilities Act (ADA)* prohibits discrimination against an individual because of disability and requires larger businesses (fifteen or more employees) to provide reasonable work accommodations for an employee with disabilities whenever feasible. More information can be obtained on-line at *www.usdoj.gov/crt/ada*.

The *Family Medical Leave Act (FMLA)* entitles employees of large companies (fifty or more) to as many as twelve weeks of unpaid leave per year when needed for " serious" health or family health reasons. Other FMLA provisions include continuation of employer-provided medical coverage and restoration to the same or an equivalent job upon returning to work. More information can be obtained on-line at *www.dol.gov/elaws/esa/fmla*.

COBRA is a federal law that requires medical insurance companies to allow employees who have been laid off or become disabled to continue their group medical insurance coverage for up to eighteen months. It does not, however, control the monthly premium, which can be quite high. The potential advantage of purchasing the COBRA group plan, even when another type of coverage might be cheaper is that because the coverage provided is unbroken, there is no consideration of pre-existing medical conditions (as there might be if a new health insurance plan is sought after developing a disabling medical condition). Furthermore, our right to purchase subsequent coverage under HIPAA rules (see next paragraph) is retained when the eighteen months of COBRA coverage is exhausted. More information on COBRA can be found on-line at *www.cobrainsurance.com*.

The *Health Insurance Portability and Accountability Act (HIPAA)* limits an insurer's ability to deny medical coverage due to pre-existing conditions and makes it illegal for group health plans to discriminate on the basis of medical history. HIPAA also makes it possible for individuals whose COBRA coverage has become exhausted to convert to other, sometimes less expensive, health insurance coverage. A certificate from the insurance carrier verifying the completion of the eighteen month COBRA coverage, along with HIPAA forms that can be obtained online, can be used to purchase further coverage, *without consideration of health status*. In order to obtain the best coverage at the most reasonable rate it may be necessary to obtain quotes from a number of different health insurance companies and HMOs. More information about HIPAA protections can be obtained online at *www.hcfa.gov/medicaid/HIPAA*.

Although the federal government has taken steps to protect those of us who have become disabled from discrimination on the part of employers and insurers, enforcement of ADA, FMLA, COBRA and HIPAA regulations requires action on our part. If we feel that we have been treated unjustly, we can report the problem to our employer or insurance carrier and ask for re   If we are still dissatisfied, *a discrimination*   be filed with our state insurance comm   e fair employment agency. Federal empl   similar complaints with the *Equal Emp*   *portunities Commission (EEOC).* Formal com   *is* type often lead to an investigation and s   a negotiated settlement. If the matter canr   be resolved, a "right to sue" letter can be of   permits the filing of a civil lawsuit. In such c   will most likely be important to consult an attorney v. o specializes in civil rights law. More information regarding the EEOC can be obtained on-line at *www.eeoc.gov.*

Organizations and Agencies That Can Help

The 2-1-1 Information Line

The *2-1-1 information line* is a simple and toll-free means of obtaining information regarding community resources, especially those available to individuals with disabilities. Initially launched by the United Way and subsequently supported by bi-partisan congressional legislation, the 2-1-1 system is similar to the national 4-1-1 directory information and 9-1-1 emergency service systems. The 2-1-1 caller is immediately and directly connected to a counselor who can provide information about obtaining necessities such as basic human needs, medical resources, financial assistance, job training, education, transportation, homemaker services, programs for children and the elderly and even volunteer opportunities. At the time of my writing less than half of American cities were connected to the 2-1-1 system, but it is expected to be expanded in the near future and will, most likely, soon become nationwide.

Appendix B: Programs and Organizations that Assist the Disabled

NATIONWIDE AGENCY	CITY	TELEPHONE	EMAIL
National Disability Rights Network	Washington D.C.	202-408-9514	www.napas.org
Navajo United Way	Window Rock, AZ	928-871-6661	http://www.navajoway.org/NAPAP.html
U.S. Department of Justice Disability Rights Division	Washington D.C.	800-514-0301	www.usdoj.gov/crt/ada
U.S. Equal Opportunity Commission	Washington D.C.	800-669-4000	www.eeoc.gov
American Association for People With Disabilities		800-840-8844	www.aapd-dc.org
Social Security Administration		800-772-1213	www.ssa.gov
Government-Sponsored Benefit Programs			www.govbenefits.gov
Referral to Local Assistance Services		211	www.211.org

LOCAL AGENCY	CITY	TELEPHONE
Alabama		
Alabama Governor's Office on Disability	Montgomery	888-879-3582
Alabama Department of Rehabilitation	Montgomery	800-441-7607
Alaska		
Disability Law Center of Alaska	Anchorage	800-478-1234
American Samoa		
American Samoa Protection and Advocacy	Pago Pago	684-633-2441
Arizona		
Arizona Center for Disability Law	Phoenix	602-274-6287
Arkansas		
Arkansas Disability Rights Center	Little Rock	501-296-1775
California		
California Department of Rehabilitation	Numerous offices	800-952-5544
Community Resources for Independence	Ukiah	707-463-8875 800-528-7704 (in-state only)
California Disabled Resources Center	Long Beach	562-427-1000 x111
California Familia Unida	Los Angeles	323-261-5565 877-298-3267 (in-state only)

Legal Services of Northern California	Sacramento	916-551-2150
TODEC Legal Center	Perris	800-778-3713
California Protection and Advocacy, Inc.	Sacramento	800-776-5746
Colorado		
Colorado Center for Legal Advocacy	Denver	303-722-0300
Connecticut		
Connecticut Office of Protection and Advocacy for Persons With Disabilities	Hartford	860-297-4300
Delaware		
Delaware Community Legal Aid Society	Wilmington	302-575-0690
Florida		
Florida Abilities Inc.	Clearwater	727-538-7370 x345
Florida Advocacy Center for Persons With Disabilities	Tallahassee	800-342-0823
Georgia		
Georgia Division of Rehab. Services	Atlanta	404-657-2239
Georgia Advocacy Office	Decatur	404-885-1234
Hawaii		
Hawaii Centers for Independent Living	Honolulu	808-522-5400
Hawaii Disability Rights Center	Honolulu	808-949-2922
Idaho		
Idaho Comprehensive Advocacy, Inc.	Boise	866-262-3462
Idaho Division of Vocational Rehab.	Boise	202-334-3390
Illinois		
Illinois Equip for Equality, Inc.	Chicago	312-341-0022
Illinois Department of Human Services	Springfield	217-557-1601
Indiana		
Indiana Protection & Advocacy Services	Indianapolis	800-622-4845
Iowa		
Iowa Protection and Advocacy	West Des Moines	800-779-2502
Kansas		
Kansas Advocacy & Protective Services, Inc.	Manhattan	800-779-2502
Kentucky		
Kentucky Center for Accessible Living, Inc.	Louisville	502-589-6620
Department of Public Advocacy P&A Division	Frankfort	502-564-2967
Louisiana		
Louisiana Advocacy Center	New Orleans	800-960-7705 x481
Maine		
Disability Rights Center of Maine	Augusta	207-626-2774
Maryland		
Maryland Disability Law Center	Baltimore	410-727-6352
Massachusetts		

Massachusetts Disability Law Center	Boston	800-872-9992
Massachusetts Rehabilitation Commission	Boston	617-573-1600
Michigan		
Michigan Protection and Advocacy	Lansing	517-487-1755
Minnesota		
Minnesota Legal Aid Society	Minneapolis	612-332-1441
Minnesota Department of Economic Security	St. Paul	651-632-5108
Mississippi		
Mississippi Department of Rehabilitation	Madison	800-443-1000
Mississippi Protection and Advocacy	Jackson	601-981-8207
Missouri		
Missouri Division of Vocational Rehabilitation	Jefferson City	573-751-3251
Missouri Protection and Advocacy	Jefferson City	573-893-3333
Montana		
Montana Advocacy Program	Helena	406-449-2344
Nebraska		
Nebraska Advocacy Services	Lincoln	402-474-3183
Nevada		
Nevada Disability Advocacy Center	Las Vegas	702-257-8150
New Hampshire		
New Hampshire Disability Rights Center	Concord	603-228-0432
New Jersey		
New Jersey Protection & Advocacy	Trenton	609-292-9742
New Mexico		
New Mexico State Department of Education	Santa Fe	505-954-8523
New Mexico Protection & Advocacy	Albuquerque	505-256-3100
New York		
New York Abilities, Inc. for Disability Service	Albertson	516-465-1522
New York Neighborhood Legal Services	Buffalo	716-847-0650
New York State Commission on Quality of Care for the Mentally Disabled	Schenectady	518-388-4369
North Carolina		
Carolina Legal Assistance	Raleigh	919-856-2195
North Carolina Department of Health & Human Services	Raleigh	919-589-3563
North Dakota		
North Dakota Protection and Advocacy Project	Bismark	701-328-2950
North Dakota Rehab Services, Inc.	Minot	701-839-4240
Ohio		
Legal Services of Northwest Ohio	Defiance	419-782-1828

Ohio Linking Employment, Abilities & Potential	Cleveland	216-696-2716
Ohio Legal Rights Service	Columbus	614-466-7264
Oklahoma		
Oklahoma Disability Law Center	Oklahoma City	405-525-7755
Oregon		
Oregon Advocacy Center	Portland	503-243-2081
Pennsylvania		
Pennsylvania Protection & Advocacy	Harrisburg	800-692-7443
Puerto Rico		
Puerto Rico Office of the Ombudsman for Persons with Disabilities	San Juan	787-725-2333
Rhode Island		
Rhode Island Disability Law Center	Providence	401-831-3150
South Carolina		
South Carolina Protection & Advocacy for People with Disabilities	Columbia	866-275-7273
South Carolina Vocational Rehab Dept.	West Columbia	803-896-6500
South Dakota		
South Dakota Black Hills Special Services Cooperative	Pierre	800-224-5336
South Dakota Advocacy Services	Pierre	605-224-8294
Tennessee		
Tennessee Protection & Advocacy	Memphis	901-458-6013
Texas		
Texas Advocacy, Inc.	Austin	512-454-4816
Utah		
Utah Disability Law Center	Salt Lake City	800-662-9080
Utah State Office of Rehabilitation	Salt Lake City	801-538-7530
Vermont		
Vermont Protection & Advocacy	Montpelier	802-229-1355 x101
Virginia		
Virginia Access Independence	Winchester	540-662-4452
Virginia Association of Community Rehabilitation Programs	Alexandria	703-461-8747
Virginia Office for Protection and Advocacy	Richmond	804-225-2042
Virgin Islands		
Virgin Islands Advocacy	Frederiksted, St. Croix	340-772-1200
Washington		
Washington Employment Security Department	Olympia	360-438-3168
Washington Positive Solutions	Seattle	206-322-8181
Protection & Advocacy	Edmonds	800-562-2702
West Virginia		
West Virginia Advocates	Charleston	800-950-5250
West Virginia University Center for Excellence in Disabilities	Morgantown	304-293-4692

Appendix C: Organizations that Assist Individuals with Chronic Medical Conditions

ILLNESS	TELEPHONE	EMAIL
Alcoholism		
Alcoholics Anonymous	800-923-8722	www.alcoholicsanonymous.org
24-Hour Alcohol Helplines	800-229-7708 800-252-6465	
Anorexia		
National Association of Anorexia Nervosa	847-831-3438	
Alzheimer's		
Alzheimer's Association	800-272-3900	www.alz.org
Arthritis		
Arthritis Foundation	800-283-7800	www.arthritis.org
Asthma		
Allies Against Asthma	734-615-3312	www.asthma.umich.edu
Attention Deficit Disorder		
Children and Adults with Attention Deficit Disorders	800-233-4050	www.chadd.com
Blindness		
American Council of the Blind	800-424-8666	www.acb.org
American Foundation for the Blind	800-232-5463	www.afb.org
Braille Institute	800-808-2555	www.brailleinstitute.org
Cancer		
AMC Cancer Research Center and Foundation	800-321-1557	www.amc.org
American Cancer Society	800-ACS-2345	www.cancer.org
Chronic Fatigue Syndrome		
American Association for Chronic Fatigue Syndrome	847-258-7248	www.aacfs.org
Chronic Fatigue Syndrome Association of America	800-442-3437	www.cfids.org
National CFIDS Foundation	718-449-3535	www.ncf-net.org
Chronic Pain		
American Chronic Pain Association	800-533-3231	www.theacpa.org
Cocaine Addiction		
Cocaine Anonymous	800-347-8998	www.ca.org
Codependency		
Codependents Anonymous (CODA)	714-573-0174	www.codependents.org
Compulsive Overeating		
Overeaters Anonymous	505-891-2664	www.oa.org
Crohn's/Colitis		
Crohn's and Colitis Foundation	800-932-2423	www.ccfa.org

Diabetes		
American Diabetes Association	800-342-2383	www.diabetes.org
Diabetes Institute Foundation	757-446-8420	www.dif.org
Drug Addiction		
Narcotics Anonymous	818-773-9999	www.na.org
Emphysema		
Emphysema Foundation	816-452-3132	www.emphysema.net
Epilepsy		
Epilepsy Foundation	800-332-1000	www.efa.org
Fibromyalgia		
National Fibromyalgia Association	714-921-0150	www.fmaware.org
Heart Disease		
American Heart Association	800-242-9721	www.americanheart.org
Hemophilia		
National Hemophilia Foundation	800-424-2634	www.hemophilia.org
Hepatitis		
Health Talk Hepatitis C	206-352-4066	www.healthtalk.com
Hepatitis Foundation International	800-891-0707	www.hepfi.org
HIV/AIDS		
HIV/AIDS Treatment and Information Service	800-HIV-0440	www.HIVATIS.org
National Association of People with Aids	202-898-0414	www.napwa.org
Hypertension		
American Society of Hypertension	212-644-0650	www.ash-us.org
Incest		
Survivors of Incest Anonymous	410-282-3400	www.siawso.org
Kidney		
American Association of Kidney Patients	800-749-2257	www.aakp.org
National Kidney Foundation	800-622-9010	www.kidney.org
Liver		
American Liver Foundation	800-GOLIVER	www.liverfoundation.org
Lung		
American Lung Association	212-315-8700	www.lungusa.org
Lupus		
Lupus Foundation of America	310-670-9292	www.lupus.org
Mental Illness		
National Alliance for the Mentally Ill	800-950-NAMI	www.nami.org
Migraine		
Migraine Awareness Group	703-739-9384	www.migraines.org
Multiple Sclerosis		
Multiple Sclerosis Education Network	206-352-4066	www.healthtalk.com
Multiple Sclerosis Foundation	800-225-6495	www.msfacts.org
UCSF Multiple Sclerosis Center	415-514-1684	http://mscenter.his.ucsf.edu
Osteoporosis		
Foundation for Osteoporosis Research and Education	888-266-3015	www.fore.org

National Osteoporosis Foundation	202-223-2226	www.nof.org
Parkinson's		
American Parkinson's Disease Association	800-223-2732	www.apdaparkinson.org
Parkinson's Disease Foundation	800-457-6676	www.pdf.org
Scleroderma		
Scleroderma	800-722-4673	www.scleroderma.org
Sickle Cell		
Sickle Disease Association of America	800-421-8453	www.sicklecelldisease.org
Smoking		
Nicotine Anonymous	415-750-0328	www.nicotine-anonymous.org
Smokenders	80-828-4357	www.smokenders.com
Spinal Cord Injury		
Christopher Reeve Paralysis Foundation	800-225-0292	www.apacure.com
Foundation for Spinal Cord Injury Prevention and Cure	800-342-0330	www.fscip.org
Kent Waldrep National Paralysis Foundation	877-724-2873	
Stroke		
National Institute of Neurological Disorders and Stroke	800-352-9424	www.ninds.nih.gov
National Stroke Association	800-STROKES	www.stroke.org

Index